Praise for *Unforgettable Presence*

Unforgettable Presence is more than a career guide—it's a call to action for professionals to show up for others and themselves. Lorraine's thoughtful advice and stories will leave you feeling inspired to show up with purpose and presence every day.

—Sherrie Westin
CEO of Sesame Workshop, the nonprofit educational organization behind Sesame Street

Unforgettable Presence is a career game changer, packed with Lorraine K. Lee's expert insights on crafting a standout brand that gets you seen and recognized.

—Dorie Clark
Wall Street Journal bestselling author of *The Long Game* and executive education faculty, Columbia Business School

Unforgettable Presence is a must-read for any team aiming to build confidence, presence, and leadership skills. I'd recommend this to any leader who wants to invest in their team's growth and success, and develop a high-impact team.

—Stanley Tang
DoorDash cofounder and chief product officer

In *Unforgettable Presence,* Lorraine K. Lee shares practical steps for building a successful career in today's corporate world and shows us that leadership is a skill anyone can develop. This book is a meaningful guide for anyone ready to unlock their full potential.

—Christina Hall
chief people officer at Instacart

Lorraine K. Lee has nailed the formula for professional presence. *Unforgettable Presence* is a powerful resource for those who want to be seen, heard, and respected in any room they walk (or dial) into.

—Ross Pomerantz (aka "Corporate Bro")
entrepreneur and content creator

In a world where attention is our most precious commodity, having a strong, authentic presence is critical. Lorraine Lee provides specific, actionable advice to help all of us break through the noise and have the impact we want.

—Matt Abrahams
strategic communication lecturer at
Stanford GSB, host of *Think Fast Talk Smart the Podcast*,
and author of *Think Faster, Talk Smarter*

Working with Lorraine has always been a highlight for our teams at Cisco – her insights are practical, refreshing, and easy to put into action. *Unforgettable Presence* brings that same energy, offering leaders a toolkit for building genuine influence and impact. It's the kind of book you'll keep coming back to.

—Carlo Dela Fuente
chief of staff and director
of business operations at Cisco (Webex)

Lorraine K. Lee's *Unforgettable Presence* delivers what every ambitious professional and entrepreneur needs to thrive: a roadmap for building credibility, making an impact, and leaving a lasting impression in every interaction.

—Jason Feifer
editor in chief of *Entrepreneur* magazine

Setting yourself apart from everyone else is easier said than done. But Lorraine's insights, lessons, and the information she's gathered in this instructive manual will help anyone thrive in corporate America, entrepreneurship, and beyond.

—Angel Au-Yeung
reporter at the *Wall Street Journal* and
co-author of *Wonder Boy: Tony Hsieh, Zappos, and
the Myth of Happiness in Silicon Valley*

Lorraine Lee's *Unforgettable Presence* is the confidence boost every professional needs. A must-read for anyone ready to make their mark in the professional world.

—**Vanessa Van Edwards**
founder of ScienceofPeople.com
and best-selling author

In today's fast-evolving workplace, individuals and teams alike can benefit from the confidence and communication strategies in *Unforgettable Presence*. Lorraine Lee's tactical advice empowers leaders to help their teams stand out and succeed.

—**Robert Glazer**
Wall Street Journal and *USA Today* best-selling
author of *Elevate Your Team* & *Friday Forward*

I struggled to find and own my presence in my career. Lorraine provides a valuable roadmap on how to be simply unforgettable.

—**Mita Mallick**
Wall Street Journal and *USA Today* best-selling
author of *Reimagine Inclusion*

So much about the world of work comes down to how you show up and the impression you leave on others. Whether you're a seasoned professional or just starting out, Lorraine Lee has filled this book with the tools you need to stand out, make a difference and get ahead.

—**Andrew Seaman**
LinkedIn's editor for jobs and career development

Profound. Resonant. Transformational. A gift every mentor should offer those in their professional care.

—**H Walker**
vice president and human centered
strategies officer, Boys & Girls Clubs of America

LORRAINE K. LEE

Unforgettable Presence

Get Seen, Gain Influence, and Catapult Your Career

WILEY

Published by John Wiley & Sons, Inc., Hoboken, New Jersey.
Published simultaneously in Canada.

For general information on our other products and services or for technical support, please contact our Customer Care Department within the United States at (800) 762-2974, outside the United States at (317) 572-3993 or fax (317) 572-4002.

Wiley also publishes its books in a variety of electronic formats. Some content that appears in print may not be available in electronic formats. For more information about Wiley products, visit our web site at www.wiley.com.

Library of Congress Cataloging-in-Publication Data is Available:

ISBN: 9781394281725 (cloth)
ISBN: 9781394281732 (ePub)
ISBN: 9781394281749 (ePDF)

Cover design: Wiley
Cover image(s): © Chandan/Adobe Stock
Author Photo: © Sonia Holstein

SKY10099103_022725

For all of my family, mentors, and collaborators.

Contents

Introduction

What Does It Mean to Be Unforgettable?

I still remember how ecstatic I was when I got my first promotion, moving from "associate editor" to "news editor" at LinkedIn after only a year. It came as a surprise, but I wasn't complaining!

Of course, being the ambitious professional that I am, it wasn't long before I started thinking about how I could reach the next level.

I would work very hard for the next five years—I even moved to Hong Kong for a year to help launch one of the company's most important products to date. Despite working on big initiatives like these and always getting positive feedback from my peers, reaching that next level didn't happen for me.

I loved my job at LinkedIn and learned a ton while I was there, but something wasn't working for me, and I couldn't figure out what it was.

I did what I was told, I did it quickly, and I did it well. My peers liked me, and I worked on key projects. What was missing?

After much reflection, I had realized that my heads-down, say-yes-to-anything and deferential approach was the problem.

After six years at LinkedIn, I was presented with a new and exciting challenge at the presentation platform Prezi that would allow me to fulfill my dream of becoming a manager and build an editorial team from the ground up.

This time, I knew I wanted to approach my career differently.

It would take a new set of skills—and a major mindset shift—to start moving toward the goals I wanted for myself: more visibility, more strategic projects, and to be seen as a leader.

At Prezi, I got to work with extraordinary speakers and business leaders, learning from people whose whole career was based on their presence. I consulted widely and started to seek out sponsors and mentors. I studied "executive presence" and thought about what distinguished leaders from overlooked hard workers.

Just like at LinkedIn, I got promoted after one year. Except this time, it wasn't a surprise. I had intentionally worked my way up to becoming a director, and just as importantly, I felt like I belonged in the role.

I continued to make it my mission to be more intentional about my career growth: to ask the specific questions that would tell me exactly what decision-makers were looking for at the next level, to *ask* for the promotion (you may think your managers know you want it—they don't), and to work smarter after learning where I missed the mark in my previous role.

I called this new mindset "becoming the CEO of my own career." I knew that I couldn't just sit back and let my hard work do the talking. I had to be *intentional*, and I had to have a plan.

■　■　■

If you think someone has "presence," what qualities come to mind?

You might think they seem confident and self-assured; perhaps their poise drew you in or they had a warmth they exuded when they spoke.

While all these things can certainly define presence—and we'll discuss these qualities in the book—when it comes to a professional context, *presence has come to mean so much more.*

It's about how someone communicates, how they build relationships, and how they share feedback. It's about their reputation and how they advocate for themselves. And now, it's also about how we show up virtually on video calls (and whatever future technology becomes the next big thing), on platforms like LinkedIn, and what people say about us when we're not in the room. With so many different working environments (in-person, hybrid, and remote) and people more distracted than they've ever been, learning how to be seen and gain influence has never been more important for one's career.

Along the way I've discovered something about presence that I think others have missed—that it's about **both how *and* where you're seen.**

The majority of my career had been focused on the "how"—it was the traditional definition of presence, which included traits like how confident I appeared presenting in a room full of people and my overall reputation as a hard worker.

But as time went on and the world underwent a huge shift to virtual, there was something beyond the "how" that I realized was equally as important: the "where." This got only more pronounced during and after the pandemic, where I couldn't rely on in-person interactions to create an impression and build my reputation and brand. Instead, the most frequent and important touchpoints and interactions with my peers were moments when we *weren't* face-to-face.

That's continued to be the case for many of us. Without the metaphorical water cooler, how we show up in Slack or Teams channels (and even *which* channels we're in) has become how we create a presence among our peers. Without someone's desk to stop at, the way you show up in online meetings becomes extra important. LinkedIn has become our virtual water cooler and the ultimate virtual office. Even your email signature and profile photo on your video calls contribute to your professional presence.

I won't pretend that creating a strong presence will happen overnight, but it's certainly doable and something that can be learned. Some themes emerge: preparation, thoughtfulness, and attention to detail. Leveraging technology and connecting as humans. Each one on its own doesn't sound like a game-changer, but when you combine them all and add in a few special ingredients (like intentionality and mindset), your professional presence becomes one of your most important assets to catapulting your career and standing out in today's workplace.

■ ■ ■

The goal of this book is to be a "how to" for anyone who wants to create an *unforgettable presence*—whether you're in-person, hybrid, or virtual. If you're reading this, you're someone who's ambitious and works hard but may be getting overlooked and struggling to get recognized for the smart and brilliant leader you are and know you can be. My hope is to share the career lessons that have built my presence across key areas like communication, public speaking, and self-advocacy so you can build on what you're currently doing—and create an unforgettable presence that will help you reach the next level in your career faster, smarter, and with fewer roadblocks.

We'll cover four key sections that will help you strategically build your presence: setting a strong foundation, key skills for the modern workplace, how to approach career advancement, and what's needed to be an unforgettable leader and manager.

If you follow my work or have seen me speak, you know I'm all about tangible, actionable tips, and this book is no different. It focuses on hands-on tactics that I've tested myself and shared with millions of professionals.

While this book will have valuable insights and advice for professionals at any level, developing leaders will likely find the most value (after all, I've been in your shoes). Many of you are figuring out how to reach that next level while also training the next generation on how to succeed.

I hope this serves as an important resource for experienced leaders as well. You're tasked with training and retaining your top talent; to do that, you need to provide support and growth opportunities for your teams. A LinkedIn Learning report[1] shared that 94% of employees would stay at a company longer if it invested in their learning and development. My hope is for you to share this as a resource for your teams to inspire, motivate, and coach them on these essential workplace skills that many of us don't get taught (and I'm confident you'll pick up a new skill or best practice you can use, too!).

I'll also spend time speaking to the unique challenges that people from marginalized groups face in developing their presence. For a long time, the characteristics of success closely mirrored the competencies of a certain persona—Eurocentric, male, loud, and brimming with unbridled confidence (even if it was not always warranted).

Thankfully this is changing (you'll find some fascinating data on how in these pages), but the playbook for how women, introverts, and other underrepresented groups thrive is still being written. I know that sometimes people like us are stepping into a world that was not built for our experiences or that feels unfamiliar (and even unwelcoming). While this can be unintentional, the impacts are real and significant. Being part of an underrepresented group brings its own challenges and those have to be addressed—whether you're part of one of those groups or not—if people are going to feel comfortable stepping up and speaking freely. That's why you'll find advice from a broad range of voices in this book, in addition to my own experiences as an Asian American woman.

And while I've shared my insights on presence with millions of professionals through my work with Fortune 500 companies, my one-on-one executive coaching, my LinkedIn Learning courses, and my LinkedIn audience—I believe my voice isn't the only one you should hear.

That's why I've interviewed dozens of business leaders, content creators, and experts in their craft for this book: people like bestselling authors Daniel Pink (who has five *New York Times* bestsellers to his name, including *Drive*) and Kim Scott (author of *Radical Candor, Radical Respect,* and cofounder of Radical Candor LLC). These experts come from a broad range of industries and backgrounds: from comedians and content creators to C-suite executives at some of the world's largest companies. Each one is a master of the different skills I'll discuss, and each shares their valuable experiences. What they all have in common is a presence and expertise that have made them stand out in their field.

You'll find more than 140 of their insights and tips sprinkled throughout the book to help you on your journey to creating your own unforgettable presence.

■ ■ ■

Stepping into the spotlight—deciding to be intentional and thoughtful about your presence and opening yourself up to the judgment of others—can be intimidating, so I commend you for taking that leap! I'll be here with you every step of the way.

I'd love to know how you apply what you read here and any thoughts you want to share on the book. Please drop me a message (book@lorraineklee.com) or follow me on LinkedIn. Your feedback is invaluable, and I can't wait to hear about the progress I know you'll see when you incorporate what you learn in this book.

Part I

Building Your Foundation

Chapter 1

Crafting Your Career Brand

Before we dive into the tactical career advice and frameworks, it's important that we're first *thinking smartly* about our careers.

To do that, we need to talk about a phrase that makes many people cringe: "personal brand."

I understand why people don't like it. It can feel self-promotional, and like you're putting on a fake persona. It might seem like it's only something for social media influencers or someone trying to sell something. Clients have told me that they believe a personal brand is something reserved for people who are shameless about marketing themselves.

Here's the thing: **what if I told you that you already have a personal brand?**

In fact, we all do. Your brand is your reputation and what others say about you when your name comes up in conversation. It's the adjectives and accomplishments they associate with you when deciding whether to put you up for promotion. It's whether they *even know you exist*.

Your brand is your story, the quick summary of what you offer other people. It tells people how you can help them and why they should want to work with you. It tells your colleagues what they can depend on you for and what makes you unique.

Being thoughtful about your brand is not about being self-centered. It's not a way for you to trick people or make you sound more important than you are. It's a shorthand for other people to understand how you can help them and what makes you uniquely you.

3

Your personal brand can also be thought of as your *career brand*: it's your reputation at work. It helps people quickly understand the value that you offer and what it's like to work with you. It shapes important decisions like whether you should be part of a key project, how to share important feedback with you, or even who gets that promotion.

"Everything I do can impact my broader image: from a single line in an Instagram post to running into fans at my local dive bar," says Natalie Marshall, the content creator and advisor better known as Corporate Natalie. "I do feel like every move I make has the power to alter my public image, and how I carry myself is vital."

Developing an intentional career brand helps you influence what people say about you when you're not there. As the saying goes, "Your reputation precedes you."

You can choose two paths: take the time to craft your brand and control your story or leave it to chance and let others do it for you.

Not convinced that your career brand is that important? Let me share a story about how my reputation created visibility and opportunity for me.

■ ■ ■

I had been packing for an international trip when I heard the ping go off. The LinkedIn News team was getting ready to launch its first-ever Top Companies feature, and the team was under a tight deadline—with a ton of work still to be done thanks to a finicky new website platform.

The project lead was asked by his boss to choose someone to help him bring the project to the finish line. The person he chose? Me. I wasn't anywhere near the most experienced nor the most convenient (I was the youngest person on the team and would have to fly cross-country to New York), but my reputation as someone who could be depended on had spoken for itself. I quickly packed a separate suitcase ready to take on the challenge.

I landed in New York, and we quickly got to work uploading text and photos, copyediting, and tackling whatever last-minute fire drills popped up. I worked late into the evenings and was back in the office before the sun rose. Thankfully, we got it done.

On the day of the launch, munching on celebratory snacks, I reflected on what got me there. It was my brand, even though I hadn't recognized it at the time. People knew me as someone who was prepared, reliable, and calm under pressure.

This illustrates what Daniel Pink, author of five *New York Times* bestsellers, shared with me about how important simply doing good work is for building your brand. "I think the best way to build your own brand is just to do really, really good work all the time. I think that that is 80% of it. I'm not naive enough to think that's all that it is, but I really do think that that is 80% of it."

For most of you reading this book, you have that 80% locked down. It's that critical and nuanced 20% that can be the most challenging but remains an essential piece to ensuring you're seen as a leader. This is what we'll continue to tackle throughout this book.

The Mindset Shift: How to Become the CEO of Your Own Career

Many of us move through our careers believing certain truths. For example, "I will get promoted after three years because I will have paid my dues," or "My boss will remember my goals and do everything they can to help me get there." It's not hard to understand why: as we go through our school years, we're told what to do by authority figures in order to succeed. When we enter the working world, it can be easy to assume that there'd be at least *some* sort of clear path forward.

In reality, it's more like a roller coaster—full of exciting highs, unexpected drops, and sharp turns that you can't always see coming. While a great manager can certainly be a guiding force (and there is plenty of advice in this book for how managers can support their direct reports), *you* will ultimately care the most about your own career and be the one most invested in achieving the goals you've set out for yourself. In other words, you must think of yourself as the CEO of your own career.

When you adopt this attitude, *you* become responsible for your professional development and the opportunities you create for yourself. *You* set your own vision for your success by setting clear goals, making informed decisions, and advocating for yourself. It all comes down to *you*—and that should be an exciting feeling!

Here are just a few of the ways you can shift your mindset:

Before: Hard work alone will pay off.

After: If no one sees my work, it will be like I didn't do it. I need to actively share my accomplishments.

Before: My network will grow naturally.

After: I need to make sure I'm actively building relationships, not just when I need something.

Before: Feedback comes during annual reviews.

After: Feedback should be continuous if I want to grow faster.

Before: Promotions and raises happen with enough time.

After: I need to advocate for myself at every opportunity.

Bringing the outlook of a CEO to my career changed how I interact with people on a day-to-day basis. It made me proactive instead of passively letting things happen *to* me. It made me think more strategically about my career by being more vocal about my goals and intentional with building relationships. I began looking at company metrics and thinking about how my work connected to the bottom line. It boosted my confidence to feel more in control, and it ultimately put me in the driver's seat of my career. It allowed me to take charge of my professional presence.

How to Share Your Accomplishments Without Bragging

Most of us downplay our accomplishments to a fault. Don't get me wrong, humility is a good quality—but it's important to your career advancement, your team, and your company leaders that you learn how to talk about your successes.

If you're feeling uncomfortable vocalizing your work, think about different ways to frame the information by using these strategies:

- **Share learnings or wins that others can benefit from.** By doing this, you're helping them learn faster and avoid mistakes. At Prezi, I published a weekly newsletter highlighting the work from my team. I'd often have data scientists and engineers I rarely worked with reach out with ideas or resources after reading it.

- **Present work grounded in data and facts that align with the company's bottom line.** If you've positively impacted a company's bottom line, leadership will want to know. Bring the information to them in an easy-to-digest way. No one can argue with cold, hard facts!

(continued)

(continued)

- **Use collaborative language like "we" and "us."** When you do this, you're seen as more of a leader[1,2] (and if you use more "I" language, you're seen as more junior). It's a simple adjustment with powerful results. In that same weekly newsletter, a majority of the newsletter was taken up highlighting my team, with a few updates from myself. I believe a great leader lifts others up, and in the end, their successes are your successes, too.

If you're not sure how to communicate with the right tone, ask someone you trust for feedback. At LinkedIn, I would ask my managers to review emails before I sent them out to make sure I was framing things strategically and in a helpful way. Learning how to share your work is a skill unto itself, so be patient with yourself as you learn it.

How This Shows Up for Underrepresented Groups

For those coming from an underrepresented group, it can be difficult to adopt this mindset shift. For me as an Asian American, my culture is more communal than individualistic and teaches humility and deference to authority. My upbringing, combined with my introverted nature (*and* my desire to not mess up the opportunity I had working at my dream company), made me nervous to stand out.

Asian American Pacific Islander (AAPI) advocate Jerry Won knows all about this. He is the founder of World Class Speakers, where he often hears stories similar to mine—and knows how important it is to be visible. "While there may be many anecdotal stories of success from people who kept their head down and got promoted, the data says otherwise," Jerry shared with me. "The data should be a more credible source of decision-making evidence than anecdotes. And the data says, according to many studies, that Asian people don't get promoted as much. They leave the system."

I'm just one example of the deeper cultural barriers that can exist adopting this mindset shift. There are many professionals I've encountered, who are not part of this community, who struggle for different reasons—perhaps they're introverted or they're facing different biases.

One possible solution for those experiencing something similar is to remove the idea that a barrier even exists.

When renowned communications expert Vinh Giang first set out to become a keynote speaker in the United States, he had never heard of the phrase "bamboo ceiling"—a term that describes the challenges and barriers many Asian Americans face in a professional setting. As Vinh was building his speaking career, he was told more than once that he was facing an uphill battle because there were so few faces that looked like his on U.S. stages.

"I had a mentor who said to me, 'Look, you can choose to believe there's a ceiling, then there will be a ceiling, then now it's hard for you to break through. Or, you can follow the path of what Steve Martin says, 'I don't care what your background is; just be so good they can't ignore you.'"

We've seen from Vinh and Pink that great work is essential. What's equally essential is that next step: making sure others are *aware* of that great work.

How One CEO Turned Her Differences into an Asset

As an Asian female CEO (for tech company Webflow), Linda Tong has walked into a lot of rooms where she stuck out. But her approach to this offers a lot of insights.

Being an Asian female comes with disadvantages. There are things that I'm sure I have had to overcome. But on the flip side, it actually comes with advantages.

For me, it's all about mindset. It's thinking about where I can leverage both my strengths and weaknesses and my advantages and disadvantages to ultimately drive impact in the organization.

I've never looked at my race or gender as this thing that's been holding me back.

I think that mindset is debilitating. It just holds me back more than anything else. Being the only female Asian in the room in many situations also comes with a flip side, right?

How can I use this to my advantage? I used to work for the National Football League (NFL), and the first thing that people wondered about me was, "Does she actually like football?" I don't look like the typical football fan. So showing up as a superfan, demonstrating passion and excellence, it not only made me stand out even more, but I had a platform because I was the only one of my kind in the room.

By being able to really understand the environment I was in and figuring out where I can leverage these points where I'm standing out, it gave me a bigger platform to demonstrate where I can add value.

I took those moments where it could have been, "Oh, I don't fit in this room and I'm going to shrink to the back," and I spread my wings and really screamed and shouted.

The EPIC Career Brand

So how do you take charge of your career? You create an EPIC career brand.

Describing your brand can easily feel vague or unclear—the last thing you want is to use lots of buzzwords that don't mean anything. To make it powerful and easy to understand, your brand needs four crucial elements:

- **E**xperiences
- **P**ersonality
- **I**dentity
- **C**ommunity

The EPIC Framework is a simple way to curate how you want to present yourself and be remembered. Think of them as the essential ingredients in your brand recipe. Let's go through each element.

Experiences: This is information about your professional journey, and any life events that have influenced you. While you might have the same skills as someone else, your experiences are what make your story memorable and unique.

Personality: Your brand is not only about what you do but how you do it. These are the personality traits, soft skills, and special qualities that define who you are.

Identity: This is about your values, what you stand for, and your cultural background. Telling people about what you value helps them predict how you'll behave in just about any situation. Your values tell people how you'll show up every day.

Community: Ever heard the phrase "Perception is reality?" Your brand will depend on making sure your network sees you the way you want to be seen. How do your colleagues and former managers describe you? How do your peers perceive you on LinkedIn? We are all part of a community, and what these people say about us often carries more weight than what we say about ourselves.

This framework can give some shape to what you want to share.

Activity: *Take a moment and write down two or three things for each part of the EPIC Framework that apply to you. Do you think others see you the way you want to be seen? Do they feel like important things that people should know about you? If you're having trouble, don't worry! This is the perfect time to connect with a few trusted colleagues to get a pulse on what your reputation currently is and whether it matches up to your ideal career brand.*

Apply Your Career Brand in Four Steps

Once you understand the fundamental parts of what goes into your career brand, it's time to dig in a bit deeper. Building and evolving your career brand is something you should do throughout your working life. If that seems overwhelming, the important thing is to start small and build your brand over time.

Step 1: Decide What's Authentic for You

In crafting your career brand, it's crucial to lead with authenticity. If it feels like you're talking about an entirely different person, it will be hard for others to see you in that way. Think about each element you decided on and make sure that you feel like it honestly represents you.

"You've got to figure out how to be your authentic self, how to show up as yourself," says Kim Scott, bestselling author of *Radical Candor*. "Make sure that you're having a positive impact without losing yourself. It's useful to have real human relationships at work because that will create a feeling that it's safe for you to show up as you are."

There's no question that authenticity has become the default expectation in today's workplace. The pandemic normalized behaviors that used to be frowned upon—like showing people the inside of your home (even if it's messy), talking openly about mental health, and taking days off when you need them.

Authenticity has also become a critical quality for today's leaders. In a 2012 survey of U.S. business executives,[2] authenticity did not even register as an important trait in business leaders. A decade later, it had rocketed up the rankings to become one of the top five communication skills required of leaders (and the second-highest rated trait when it comes to appearance). As the study says, "Nowadays, to be seen as leadership material, executives are expected to reveal who they fundamentally are."

It can be particularly hard to feel comfortable being authentic when you grew up in a different culture, but it's no less important. "You will get to a certain level following the dominant culture, you even can make it to a leadership position. But I can attest from personal experience that there will be a point in your career where that's not going to work anymore," says Joey Aviles, a transformational keynote speaker and lead researcher.

Joey shared a story with me about how when interviewing for a senior role with a conservative organization, he became afraid to show his authentic self. He used to wear a pair of bright red eyeglasses but, afraid of being judged, he left them in his car during the interviews.

Crafting Your Career Brand

He got the job, but after a few months—during a tense time—he decided that he couldn't hide part of himself and succeed.

"I needed to show up as Joey 1000%. One morning I said, 'Enough hiding.' I brought those red eyeglasses, I combined them and matched them with a red bow tie, and walked into my first meeting," he told me. "We doubt ourselves and we hide our true point of view because we are afraid of being judged or mistreated. But we also minimize our brilliance in the workplace. With the red eyeglasses came my true talents in the workplace, my true thoughts and approaches."

So how do you define what's authentic for you?

Remember that your career brand isn't just about your skills—it's also about your story. If you have expertise in your domain, chances are that everyone around you also has those "hard" skills. What sets you apart is your soft skills and your experiences. Think about things like these:

- **Your superpower:** What do you do a little differently, or a little better, than everyone else? What do people often come to you for help with? What really energizes you? Think broadly about what makes you stand out and what you want to be known for. Your superpower should be something that resonates with you, not a mold you're trying to fit into of what you think other people value.

- **What's unique(ish) about you:** People can get caught up in worrying about if something is truly unique, so "unusual" may be a better measuring stick. The key here is to lean into your story to identify what is both memorable and useful for your audience. Do you have an experience that few others have had? A personality trait that may be underrepresented in your field?

- **How you became who you are:** Part of your career brand should leverage what has brought you success so far. It could be about a pivotal experience you had at work or your cultural background. It should tell people about your journey and how it helped you get to where you are today.

Conquering Imposter Syndrome

One big obstacle to improving your presence in your workplace is imposter syndrome—that all too common feeling where you doubt your capabilities or feel like you don't belong in a certain room because you think others are smarter. It was identified in the 1970s when women, who were achieving new heights in the workplace, began telling their therapists that they felt like they didn't deserve their positions.[3] It's something that can be a real barrier to taking ownership of your career and letting others know about all the fantastic work you're doing.

Psychologists describe classic signs of imposter syndrome as having three major characteristics:

- Thinking that people have an exaggerated view of your abilities
- The frequent tendency to downplay your achievements
- The fear of being exposed as a fraud

It's completely natural to have imposter syndrome, but there are many ways you can implement a mindset shift to not let it consume you. Daniel Pink puts it this way: "Impostor syndrome suggests that you're worse than everybody else, which is fundamentally empirically not true. Everybody is struggling. And, I don't

(continued)

(continued)

want to sound like a Hallmark card, but there is this tendency to compare our insides to everybody else's outsides. And that's a game you can never win."

You can also reframe your perspective by talking about your worries with people you trust. You'll quickly realize that almost everyone has these feelings (it may be reassuring for you to learn that many of the executives I interviewed for this book have experienced it)—but the people who stand out and reach their goals are the ones who push through that discomfort to grow.

Think of it this way: I often share that those who experience imposter syndrome should feel proud of themselves. This feeling often creeps up when we're put in uncomfortable situations, and those are the situations we grow most in. If you were always the smartest person in the room, you wouldn't learn much and life would be pretty boring!

Step 2: Plan **Where** *You Show Up*

A really common mistake I see is that people decide what their career brand is and think that they're done. But, as I explained in the introduction, the **where** of presence is just as important as the how.

Think about all the different touchpoints you have with people during the week. For most people, the list is the same: email, chat, meetings, LinkedIn, and in-person interactions.

Each of these can seem like a small part of your presence, but collectively they have a big impact by creating consistency and giving you a wider reach. I recommend that you do an inventory of these common touchpoints and ask yourself: Am I showing up the best way I can in this medium? Is my brand coming through clearly for people?

Maybe it's improving your email signature by adding a photo or creating a less generic out-of-office message. Maybe it's adding information about you to your Slack or Teams profile (your unique, powerful introduction [UPI] from the upcoming step 4 will work well for this).

The point is that your career brand is not an artifact that sits in a folder somewhere. You have to share it and consciously apply it in your everyday life. The more places you do that, the more people's understanding of what you offer will be transformed.

"It's always important to recognize that changing your brand takes more repetitions in people's minds than you think is necessary," says Dorie Clark, bestselling author of *The Long Game*. "In politics, there was always a saying that a voter needs to hear your name seven times before they'll remember it ... people are busy, they're distracted. You have to think about how to create an echo chamber to remind them."

Step 3: Decide How You Want to Be Seen

Part of developing your brand is understanding the difference between how your colleagues see you now and how you want them to see you in the future. Once you're aware of that gap, you can figure out what steps you need to take to get from where you are today to where you want to be.

Here's a simple thing you can do. Divide a piece of paper into two columns. On the left, write down all the adjectives that you think people would use to describe you. Don't worry too much about whether they're the "right" adjectives; just jot down what first comes to mind.

On the right, write down all the adjectives that describe how you *want* to be seen by others. You want to make things achievable (maybe you can't be "the world's top authority" right away), but it's okay to dream a little. You can still aim to be recognized for your "integrity" or be "highly respected," for example.

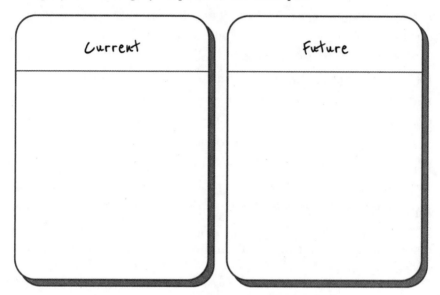

When I do this exercise with teams, many people find it easier to know aspirationally how they want to be seen in the future but aren't quite as sure about how they're being seen now. In that case, it's useful to turn to at least 10 people whom you trust—a manager, close colleagues, or friends and family. Here are some questions you can ask them:

- What are my strengths?
- What are my weaknesses?
- When do I seem most/least confident?
- What are five words you would use to describe my personality?

You can also go through past performance reviews and see if you spot any trends.

Self-reflection can sometimes be a challenge, but going through the steps can really help you become more aware of what your brand is today. It can also help you understand what other people *aren't* seeing and if there are any red flags you need to address. If you've always thought of yourself as an "analytical thinker" or "someone who brings people together" and no one mentions that, that's a great clue about how the story you tell yourself may be different from the one that others tell about you.

Step 4: What's Your UPI?

Once you've defined the key elements of your career brand and the words you use to express it, you can put all your hard work into action by coming up with your unique, powerful introduction.

We've all had to introduce ourselves at some point—whether to clients, an executive, or strangers at a networking event. Most of us will respond with some variation of: name, job title, years at company.

While it's factual, it's not putting you in the best light. You want your introduction to be a launching point for someone to learn more about you or know how they can turn to you in the future. Introductions are one of the most important situations in which we can create a strong impression and presence, but so many people let this opportunity pass them by.

Keynote speaker Rich Mulholland puts it succinctly. "What would I say that would make me interesting to somebody else I met? If you can't think of a reasonable answer for that, that's something that you should remedy."

As a former rock 'n' roll roadie, Rich has a very memorable UPI. While we don't all have such an exciting background to draw on, we do all have unique experiences that we can share.

Whatever your UPI is, you need to use it and test people's reactions. You can evolve what you say over time, but these are some typical key points:

- Explaining the problem you solve
- Explaining who your target audience is
- Explaining what your success metrics and goals are
- Explaining in more detail what you actually do day-to-day

Let's look at an example.

When I was at Prezi, I interacted with dozens of thought leaders. My role was very external facing, and initially I'd introduce myself with this: "Hi, I'm Lorraine. I lead the editorial team."

When I decided to create my UPI, it turned into: "Hi, I'm Lorraine, and I lead the editorial team. Our focus is to collaborate with business leaders to create content that educates and inspires our millions of users."

With this new phrase, I told people who I was, what I actually did, and I added more credibility by sharing the scope and reach of my work. I certainly felt more confident saying it, too.

You can also include something personal—like where you live, that you're a dog mom, or that you love to bake. It's important to find those moments of human connection—you never know what you may have in common with someone.

Once you've come up with your UPI, don't just use it in meetings. It can be something that informs your elevator pitch—a way to introduce yourself at parties, networking events, or anytime you meet someone new in a professional context.

What Your Brand Should Do

A common mistake is defining your brand around your current company or role. While these are things that can be part of your brand, they shouldn't be the *only* thing.

It may sound counterintuitive, but being known for things outside of your title and company benefits both you *and* your company. When others know you for what makes you unique and special, other opportunities open up, like being interviewed for articles or getting invited to speak on panels. When this happens, it's free organic brand awareness for the organization where you work, as well as amazing visibility for you, too. This is exactly what happened to me—by raising my profile externally, I also became more visible and created a strong brand inside my organization, too. (You'll learn how to do this in the next chapter.)

Ready to get started building your career brand? Download the **Career Brand Growth Kit** for a step-by-step worksheet (unforgettablepresencekit.com).

Discussion Questions

1. How would you describe your current career brand?

2. Who are you going to ask for feedback on your brand?

3. What are the first steps you want to take to update your career brand?

4. What mindset changes do you need to make to embrace your career brand?

5. Who have you seen at work or on LinkedIn who has a personal brand that you admire? What do you like about it?

Chapter 2

Turning Video Into Your Superpower

When my former student and coaching client Ivana came to me to learn how to improve her video communication skills, she—like many of us—had been spending a lot of time on video. As the founder of a healthcare start-up, she was often on calls with patients. She was also preparing for a high-stakes presentation to pitch her company, with the hopes of becoming a Stanford Fellow—and she had only three minutes to make her case.

For Ivana, a non-native English speaker who had recently moved to the United States, knowing how to show up well on video was important for increasing her confidence and showing up as her best self.

"It's little things that play a big role in terms of confidence," says Ivana. "When you see yourself and you're looking good, you're sounding good, it helps a lot."

The often-daily interactions we have over video deeply affect how we communicate our presence. While many of us have gotten more comfortable simply being on video, that doesn't mean we're doing it well. In fact, I've done many live lightning-round coaching sessions during team trainings where I give feedback on attendees' video presence. Most people have something that can be improved.

"First impressions are a big deal," says Doc Rock, director of strategic partnerships at Ecamm. "I always thought it was funny when you're trying to tell somebody something really, really important, but your laptop is on your lap and you're pointing the camera up your nose in bad lighting and built-in AirPods."

Doc makes an important point. If you're connecting with someone remotely, that video call is often the *only* way that person sees you. The impression you create on video—which has fewer signals than an in-person interaction—carries a lot of weight. Research on virtual first impressions shows that they are long lasting and slow to change,[1] so a lot can depend on these signals.

"Connection through video is not going away," says Rock. "It's amplifying and amplifying."

You may not realize that there are a lot of things you can do to tip the scales in your favor. I've collected best practices, around everything from equipment to habits to lighting tips, that will subtly and not-so-subtly influence how you're perceived on camera. It's called the TEA Method, and if you can follow it, it will become one of your biggest competitive advantages.

TEA stands for **tech, energy,** and **aesthetics**. It covers all the essential things you should do to prepare for a video call so that you come away looking both confident and competent. Many of the following suggestions are missed opportunities that others rarely take the time for. If you do, you'll reap the benefits of a natural on-camera warmth and a stronger professional presence.

Tech: The Right Tools for the Job

Technology can be one of the more overwhelming aspects of our virtual worlds. We have a lot of things to think about, and there is a lot you *can* do, but that doesn't mean you *have* to do it all.

In this next section, I'll share the essentials you need for a high-quality video call that won't break the bank.

Microphones

If you can improve only one thing, make sure your audio is crisp and clear. If the sound is good, the person on the other side of the video will be able to stay engaged no matter how bad your video is. Many people will forgive bad cameras, but they won't forgive bad audio.

This is why I recommend buying an external microphone. The microphones inside our laptops are not great. Your sound is automatically going to be crisper and richer with an external mic, and you can adjust the volume and other settings to ensure you have the best sound for *your* voice.

Product Recommendations

I have favorite products that I recommend for many aspects of the TEA Method, but technology changes fast. If you want to grab your Video Presence and Tools Checklist, in addition to my latest recommendations and special discounts, check out unforgettablepresencekit.com.

Webcams

External cameras are also another excellent investment. Our laptop webcams make us look grainy and dark, which means you're rarely looking your best once you hit "Join Meeting."

When I bought an external camera, I instantly felt more confident. I looked sharper and crisper, and external cameras do a better job of picking up lighting because they have larger sensors and better lenses. It was amazing what this simple change did to my appearance.

Camera Framing Tricks to Make You Look Like a Pro

Making sure you have the right framing is key when creating the perfect camera setup for video calls—and, you can do this for free.

Frame yourself correctly. This means three to five fingers worth of space between the top of your head and the top of the video frame, and about half of your torso showing as well. Doing this allows you to fill up more of the frame while giving space for your hand gestures to show, making it feel more like an in-person conversation. Avoid having your head take up a majority of the frame.

Position your camera at eye level. Adjust your camera so that it's level with your eyeline. The problem I most often see is cameras being too high up, which makes your presence smaller and makes the other person feel like they're looking down on you.

Energy: Your Attitude Determines Your Altitude

What sort of energy do you bring on video calls? Are you upbeat and positive, or are you having trouble focusing and disengaged because you've had so many back-to-back calls?

As we mentioned earlier, first impressions are an important part of establishing your presence and people form a first impression quickly. Estimates vary, but it takes no more than 7 seconds and can be as little as 1/10 of a second.[2] The good news is that you can positively influence this impression—and how attentive others are on the call—through your energy.

People often think that energy is like a light switch, something you can easily turn off and on. But summoning energy that others will see takes conscious effort and practice.

"It feels fake, and it feels like an act, when you haven't mastered the version of you that is higher energy," says communications expert Vinh Giang. "So if you wait up until that virtual call and then you do the higher energy version of you, it's like showing up to a saxophone concert and then playing and practicing during the performance."

That means practice and intentionality are key to getting your energy right.

Put On a Friendly Face

Do you have RBF?

RBF (also known as "resting business face" among other things) is most people's default when they hop on a video call.

When we're not in-person and we're comfortable at home, it's natural for us to be less energetic. This can be particularly true for introverts, as we don't typically project energy the way an extrovert does.

However, your mood does matter. Even through video, people can sense if we're feeling drained from back-to-back meetings or tired and uncomfortable.

I have three simple techniques I use to boost the energy that I bring to the screen:

- **Smile.** Smiles are contagious! Smiling to the other person signals that you're friendly and approachable and that it will be a positive conversation. It's a quick antidote to RBF.

- **Make yourself laugh.** Before signing onto your next video call, think of a memory or a scene from a show that makes you laugh (or if you have time, watch it!). That positive energy will be palpable to other people.

- **Use your hands.** Make sure your hands are visible on-screen. Annie Murphy Paul, author of *The Extended Mind*, cites research showing that recall of an anecdote increased by 33% if it was accompanied by hand gestures.[3,4]

Don't Mute Your Energy

Have you noticed that many people look like they are completely uninterested or disengaged when they're on mute? Their face goes blank or you can tell from their (lack of) eye contact that they're scrolling through their other tabs.

As Vanessa Van Edwards from Science of People pointed out to me, you can still be charismatic while on mute. By using "vocal affirmations"—expressions like nodding, smiling, or laughing that show that you're still interested and following along—you can show that you care about what that person is saying. Remember, even when you're on mute, people can still see you!

Make Eye Contact

When we meet someone in person, we make eye contact and shake hands to boost oxytocin, a hormone that is important for social bonding.

On video, we lose the handshake, but we can still leverage eye contact to help us connect. Making a conscious effort to look directly into the camera (or right below it, depending on your setup) will make the other person feel like you are making eye contact with them.

However, looking at your camera rather than the other person's gaze can feel unnatural. Here's what can help:

- **Turn off self-view:** Leaving it on is like putting up a mirror to yourself all day. It's exhausting! And it draws your attention away from whom you should really be paying attention to. This is a major cause of video fatigue.

- **Get an external webcam and place it on your main monitor:** I *still* get on video calls where the person's main monitor is off to the side, requiring them to look away from me the whole conversation. While I technically know we're in a conversation, part of me can't help but feel disconnected. It's like someone is talking to me while looking at their phone. It just feels *off*.

Bonus Tip: Having trouble feeling connected while looking at your camera? Try adding a photo of your loved ones on the wall behind your camera or shrink your video conferencing screen and move it to the top of your monitor right below your camera. You can also check out one of my favorite products in the Video Presence and Tools Checklist mentioned earlier that allows me to make eye contact *while* looking at the other person's face at the same time—a game-changer in keeping me engaged.

Power Up with Small Talk

Have you ever been on a call like this?

Person A: Hi! How are you today?

Person B: I'm great! How are you doing?

Person A: Good, thanks! How are you? (*awkwardly mumbles after realizing they already asked me*)

Person B: (*awkwardly chuckles*)

(I've been Person B—and can you believe this has happened more than once?)

Person A was *clearly* on autopilot, going through the motions. While this is an extreme example, being on autopilot is all too common.

It's easy to vilify small talk, but the thing is that small talk is actually a *good thing*—it's how we connect with one another, build relationships, and ease into a conversation. The problem is when we don't put any thought into our small talk and go into autopilot mode.

If we want to stand out and be seen, we need to stop doing what everyone else is doing. Instead of asking generic questions like "How are you?" or "How's the weather?" or "Can you see/hear me?" try something that will make people think about their answer.

Here are a few of my favorite alternatives that don't elicit a generic, "Good, thanks! How about you?":

- "It's so great to see you! I can't wait to hear about everything you've been working on lately. I hear you're working on Project X. How's that going?"

- "What was the highlight of your weekend?"

- "Are you watching any interesting shows? What do you recommend?"

These slight shifts in your approach have a number of benefits:

- You become more interesting to talk to (I've always appreciated the person who knows how to break up an awkward silence at the start of a call).

- They jolt the other person out of giving autopilot responses, requiring them to engage on a deeper level with you (which in turn builds stronger relationships).

- You learn more about one another and make small talk a strategic moment instead of a throwaway one.

Likewise, try to go beyond simple answers when you're asked a question. When a senior leader asks at the start of a call, "How are things going?" don't just say "Great!" and leave it at that. Take 30 seconds to offer details on the work you've been doing and its impact. Be as specific as you can—try saying something like "Things are going well! I'm really excited that we've seen a 30% increase in sign-ups this month after the changes we made to the home page copy."

A lot of people worry that they ramble when they're uncomfortable, which is why I like the "20-second rule." When you've been talking for approximately 20 seconds, try to finish your thought. That gives the other person a chance to respond. When it's your turn, ask follow-up questions to show that you're listening and interested in what they're saying.

Small talk is also a chance to find out what you have in common with the other person. "Small talk is information gathering that, if done right, is a prelude to getting you to deeper conversational topics," says Dorie Clark, bestselling author of *The Long Game*. "You just don't know what they are yet because you don't know anything about the person. It's a fishing expedition."

Thought starter: Think about some questions you might use at the start of your next call to bring the energy. Write them down and put them next to your webcam, or on your computer somewhere, so you can remember them on your next call.

Grab your "Small Talk Conversation Starters" at unforgettablepresencekit.com.

Use People's Names to Make Them Feel Included

It's the simplest thing, but remember to use the name of the person you're speaking with. People love hearing their names (and don't be afraid to ask someone if you're pronouncing it correctly if you're unsure; contrary to what many believe, my experience time and time again has shown that people appreciate when you care enough to double check). It makes us feel a sense of belonging and more connected with the person we're talking to—it's like a cheat code for building trust. If their energy is flagging, it also recaptures their attention if they're zoning out and brings their focus back to the call.

Aesthetics: Putting Yourself in the Best Light

Aesthetics are not just about how you look on camera but also how the world looks around you. It includes lighting, your environment, and your clothing. All of these things combine to influence your presence and how others see you.

Perfect Your Lighting

Believe it or not, your confidence can be greatly affected by your lighting choices. The good news is that lighting is easy to set up with the right tools, but for whatever reason it's often an afterthought for people. That won't be the case for you!

Good lighting is going to make you look fresher and more professional. Inexpensive tools can make a big difference:

- **Ring lights:** Ring lights are a strip of LED lights in the shape of, well, a ring. They help you look good by creating an even, flattering light that minimizes shadows. They should each ideally be at least a foot to 16 inches in diameter. This ensures you are getting ample light for your setup.

- **Soft box:** People usually see these in photo studios. These can work well if you're experiencing a ring light glare in your glasses because the light is softer and diffused.

- **Natural light:** For those who are lucky enough to have windows in their workspace, natural light is going to make you look the best. (And it's free!).

No matter what light source you choose, remember that it needs to come from the front—if the light is behind you, the shadows will make you look backlit.

Curate Your Environment

Having a well-thought-out environment is your chance to share a bit of your personality while still projecting a professional image. Your environment can influence how others perceive you a surprising amount. A 2020 survey of 465 professionals[5] found that 60% of people believed your background was important, compared to only 40% who felt the same about what you wear—leading to video backgrounds being called "the new business suits."

While you may have seen beautiful elaborate setups by podcasters and the like, having a simple, curated background will serve your purpose. Try to find a space with a wall relatively close behind you. This is your blank slate. Then, figure out what you want to add. A 2023 study on how "Zoom backgrounds affect trust and competence"[6] found that plants and bookcases produced the most positive reactions. I also encourage you to add things that can help people learn more about you. For example, I've met people with eye-catching wallpaper they've painted themselves, LEGO sets they've built, and interesting art. They've all been conversation starters and allowed us to break free from those pesky autopilot conversations.

What you want to avoid is mess and clutter. This can be tricky if you're in a small space. A creative way to create the appearance of a dedicated workspace is to get a room divider. I had a coworker who hung up a curtain behind him while sitting in front of his kitchen pantry, which was a great way to make things look more professional.

Note: With the advances we have seen (and will continue to see) in technology, it's not just about the background anymore. There are a number of apps and programs that allow you to bring visuals (like your name or company logo) and other interactive elements onto the screen with you to create a more immersive and visually engaging experience. These are part of your virtual presence and are a surefire way to separate what you're doing from what everyone else is doing.

What About Virtual Backgrounds?

One of the questions I get asked most often during team trainings is whether virtual backgrounds are okay to use. My answer is "Don't do it" if you can avoid it.

Our brains are already in cognitive overdrive on video, trying to parse facial cues and body language.[7] Add in the lag from virtual backgrounds—and things like moving hands popping in and out of existence—and it can be a significant distraction that undermines your presence. The technology may get better someday (a green screen will help fix a lot of these issues), but it's not there yet.

I'd also recommend avoiding blurred backgrounds. For some people a blurred background suggests that you have something to hide—that you're not where you say you are (did you sneak off to Hawaii?) or your room is a mess.

Of course, there are many exceptions to this recommendation. In general, aim to ground your virtual space with a real-world backdrop as much as you can to create a more authentic and natural interaction.

Clothes Still Matter

Style is obviously a very personal expression of your image, but there are a few simple rules of thumb for looking good on camera:

- **Aim for "jewel tone" colors:** These are richly saturated hues named for gems—think sapphire blue, ruby red, or emerald green. These colors really pop on camera.

- **Don't blend in:** Avoid colors that are too similar to your skin tone or your background. For example, you don't want to wear a white shirt in front of a white wall.

- **Avoid patterned tops:** Herringbones, plaids, checks, and especially stripes can be distracting. Stripes are particularly bad because of something called a "moiré pattern." If the pixel lines on your screen are not aligned with the stripes on your clothing, the stripes on your shirt will look like they're moving.

- **Sweatpants are fine:** Unless you're planning to show off your dance moves on camera, no one is likely to see what you're wearing below the waist. While some people will feel more confident with their full outfit on, I've given plenty of talks where I wore sweatpants to stay comfortable.

- **Context matters:** The question of how much to "dress up" depends very much on who you're meeting with and the norms of your industry. If you're meeting with a potential new client, it makes sense to put your best foot forward. If it's a weekly check-in with a coworker you've known for years, there's nothing wrong with being a little more casual.

Video Is the Present, but What About the Future?

Presence is always evolving, and video won't always be the most important interface. It's important to keep up with technology and think of how it will change your presence.

As a workplace futurist and the author of *Deep Talent*, Alexandra Levit spends a lot of time thinking and researching about how the office is changing. She is convinced that the "metaverse" will bring major changes to how we communicate and think about presence.

"Virtual reality will be the way that we conduct work in the future. It will probably start in about five years, when the technology becomes more immersive and accessible," she says. "That will affect your presence, too. All of a sudden, you'll have a digital presence that you can make anything you want, but then how do you connect that to you as a human?"

Making A Strong Impression In Person

While this chapter focuses on how important your video presence is, there will be times where we need to make a strong impression in person. For some of us, readjusting to the in-person office experience was difficult. If you only see colleagues in the flesh a day or two a week (or maybe even just at a retreat or conference), it can feel like we've forgotten how to interact naturally with people like we used to do.

There are bookshelves full of advice on how to have a strong in-person presence, but I like to focus on a few important pieces.

Body Language

Comedians know more than most people that your body language tells a story before you even say a word. When comedians walk up on stage, people are already making judgments about them even before they reach the microphone.

"What are you saying without saying anything?" asks stand-up comedian and TV writer Fumi Abe, who has performed on many big stages, including on *The Tonight Show*, on *The Late Show*, and as an opener for comedian Ronny Chieng. "What are you wearing? What's your facial expression? To me, presence is communication without using words."

Your body language will tell people how confident you are in a given situation, so you want to convey that you feel comfortable. You'll want to follow common advice like standing up straight, keeping hands out of pockets, and avoiding fidgeting.

What's even more helpful is knowing what movements to avoid that many of us are prone to do subconsciously, like these:

- **Crossed arms:** To us, it may be a self-soothing hug or habit. To others, it can signal you're defensive, upset, or uncomfortable in the situation.

- **The "dead fish" handshake:** This is a very weak and limp handshake that I experience far too often at networking events, even from senior leaders. A weak handshake can easily make others think you lack confidence and authority.

- **The laptop barrier:** Holding your laptop or notebook against your chest can seem like you're putting up a wall or trying to shield yourself.

While it's important to notice these things in yourself, be aware of these in others as well. It can be a helpful indicator to their feelings about your conversation or how comfortable they feel with you— and then you can adjust accordingly.

Manage Your Energy

One thing that many introverts struggle with is getting used to spending a lot of time around other people. While extroverts often gain energy from being around others, introverts' energy can run low after several hours (or fewer) in social situations. That's because introverts are often observing and processing more of what goes on around them, which causes them to run out of energy more quickly in loud or busy situations.

If this happens to you, it's important to know how to replenish that energy. Here are a few things you can try:

- Space out your meetings so that there's some "downtime" in between.

- Use headphones to block out distractions (and signal to others that you're not free for conversation).

- If you have an office, close your door when you need to; otherwise, find a quiet space you can go to work without distraction.

- If you're able to, get outside and go for a walk (especially in nature); many people find that doing so can reduce anxiety and reset their energy levels.[8]

Surprisingly, doubling down on trying to have a good conversation can often be just the jolt of energy you need. We're wired to be rewarded for social behaviors, so creating a genuine connection with someone can trigger a flood of serotonin and endorphins. I think we all know instinctively how energizing a great conversation can be. So even if you're not feeling very social when the conversation begins, you may walk away far more energized than when you started.

Discussion Questions

1. What technology should I invest in to make me look more professional on camera?

2. How can I better prepare for meetings so that I'm bringing enthusiasm and positive energy to the call?

3. What can I do to improve how I approach small talk with my colleagues?

4. What steps will I take to improve the aesthetics of my video calls?

5. What adjustments do I need to make to ensure that I come across as confident and energetic in my in-person interactions?

Chapter 3

Using LinkedIn the Right Way

When Mark was at a networking event for venture capital and tech start-ups, he was excited about all the new connections he was making. After a fruitful discussion with a fellow attendee, he asked to connect with her on LinkedIn. As she unlocked her phone, he got ready to spell out his name—that is, until she flashed her phone at him: her phone wallpaper was her LinkedIn "scan" code, a feature that LinkedIn members can use to help others find and connect with them more easily.

While not everyone will have LinkedIn scan codes readily available on our phone wallpaper, Mark's story illustrates a larger trend: most of us will go to LinkedIn before trying to find someone's personal website or a business page. It has become one of the most important platforms for professionals. As of the writing of this book, the site has 1 billion members, with nearly half of them active every month. At least 10 million members are C-suite level executives.[1]

Here's where most employers *and* employees get it wrong, though. They think of LinkedIn only as a place to get a job. Although it's still definitely a place to do that (seven people are hired every minute on LinkedIn[2]) or announce your promotion, it's become so much more: a landing page to tell people about yourself, the universal virtual office, and your virtual water cooler. The platform's focus on content, community, and conversations has given all of us an opportunity to shape our online presence in even bigger ways. In fact, I've worked with many professionals who have experienced firsthand that the platform is just as important for boosting their presence with their coworkers as it is with people outside their company.

Just as we form a quick impression of someone after meeting them in person, the same can be said about someone's online presence. One of my favorite stats is by the RAIN Group, and it states that 82% of buyers will look up a seller on LinkedIn before replying to a seller's outreach.[3] While we aren't all sellers, this desire to understand someone's legitimacy by checking out their LinkedIn profile is something many of us can relate to.

Ultimately, if you optimize how you set up and use LinkedIn, it will accelerate your career. It can be the bedrock of your career brand, strengthen your overall presence, and connect you with people you might have never otherwise met.

I learned this lesson very early. In fact, it was my LinkedIn profile that helped me land a job at LinkedIn!

LinkedIn had always been my dream company to work for. When a few years out of school I saw an open role that fit my experience, I excitedly applied. I was even more excited when I met Brian, a LinkedIn employee, at a barbeque soon after (he would eventually become chief of staff to the CEO, although neither of us knew it at the time!). After letting him know I applied to LinkedIn, he (naturally) looked me up on the site while I nervously stood there, hoping my profile passed the test. He was blown away. Content wasn't yet available on the platform, but profiles certainly were. And mine was *thorough*. That chance encounter got me pushed quickly through the interview process (they were already on their third round of interviews with other candidates), and a few weeks later I landed my dream job. Since then, my LinkedIn presence has landed me other amazing opportunities (including writing this book!) and given me the credibility to reach out to leaders and experts to collaborate with in my corporate role. I'm excited for you to see similar success.

Let's start off by tackling your LinkedIn profile.

Optimizing Your Profile

Profiles are the foundation of LinkedIn. As previously mentioned, they're often the first place that people go to learn more about you (even before your website), so it's important that it's complete and optimized. The good news is that, according to LinkedIn, pages with complete information get 40% more weekly views.

There are a lot of elements to your profile, but we'll focus on three critical components.

Your Experience

This is the closest thing to your résumé, so it will be a focus for people trying to learn more about you. Often people who are interested in working for your company—or who may be in the interview process—check out potential colleagues on LinkedIn, so you want to accurately depict the company and your role.

Focus on fleshing out three key areas: responsibilities, context, and metrics. Include a specific and detailed list of your responsibilities for each role, the context behind projects and your team, and your most important accomplishments (with as much data as possible) for each. If the company isn't a household name, you may also want to share a few lines about who the company is for additional context.

You don't need to include every experience you've ever had. Focus on *relevant* roles that contribute to your career brand and the story you want to tell others. If you're a few years into the workforce, you may also want to think about removing past experiences like former internships that can make you seem less experienced.

About Section

This is where you can really lean into your story. Talk about your journey and share more about yourself as a person. Explain what motivates you and what people can expect if they work with you. It's important to incorporate all the key parts of your career brand here. Most people miss the opportunity to humanize themselves by sharing their story and instead will use a generic bio that someone could find on a company website.

What really sets a good About section apart is sharing your personality rather than regurgitating your résumé (although you can still highlight a few key accomplishments). It can be about your journey, what you've learned along the way, or what excites you today. While this will help people connect with you, the keywords you use will also help you rank higher in search results for both Google and LinkedIn.

Headline

This is another missed opportunity for many people. Most people's headlines will simply be their current job title and company. This may be accurate, but it's a generic format and certainly doesn't add anything special to your presence.

Over the years, LinkedIn has increased the number of characters allowed, and I encourage you to use as many of them as possible. At a minimum, you want to include your job title, current company, and any keywords or skills that you want to show up in search results (this will make you more discoverable on both Google and LinkedIn). If you've previously worked for a well-known company, including that in your headline can increase your credibility (for example: "Ex-LinkedIn"). Think about including a mission statement or encapsulation of your career brand. (Remember those unique, powerful introductions [UPIs] from Chapter 1? Lean on those as a starting point!)

A simple formula for this mission statement is: "I help [audience] do [an action] so they can [achieve an outcome]." Here are some examples:

- "I help sales teams streamline their operations so they can increase profitability and collaborate more effectively."
- "I help mid-level managers improve their leadership skills so they can advance their careers and inspire their teams."
- "I help nonprofit organizations refine their fundraising techniques so they can secure more donations and make a greater impact."

Photos

Humans are visual beings, so tackling your profile and background photos will be critical.

For the profile picture, aim for quality. This doesn't mean you need to hire a professional photographer. You can achieve amazing results on your smartphone in front of the right setting. Aim to have a Duchenne Smile. A Duchenne Smile looks more authentic and makes you look more approachable because you "smile with your eyes," which makes the corners wrinkle up with crow's feet.

Crinkled eyes

Lifted cheeks

The background cover photo of your profile is one of the first things that people see—not to mention it's one of the biggest pieces of real estate on your page. I'm always surprised when I see generic stock images or, worse, no image at all.

The most common ones I see are nature-scape photos. Those don't share much about you unless you're the photographer who took that photo.

When thinking about what to include in your banner image, think about including one (or all) of these things:

- A clear call-to-action
- A pain point you can solve for your audience
- The value you bring to whomever you're working with

Free Templates for the Perfect Banner

I believe in the importance of a good background image so much that I've worked with a professional designer on my team to create free templates that you can download and customize. Pick your favorite and easily edit the colors, add graphics, and drag and drop photos to make it your own.

Visit unforgettablepresencekit.com to grab your 25+ free LinkedIn banner photo templates.

Recommendations

Imagine you're shown two LinkedIn profiles of individuals with similar work backgrounds; one has five glowing recommendations about their ability to lead teams and how loved they are by coworkers, and the other has zero. Who will you form a better impression of right off the bat?

I often make the analogy that LinkedIn recommendations are like Yelp for professionals. They play a huge part in social proof to potential clients, coworkers, and anyone else who's stopping by your page. Contrary to what you may think, recommendations don't have to happen only when you switch jobs. I'm a big proponent of asking for recommendations when your work is fresh in people's minds, like after a big project or speaking on a panel.

Be specific about what you're asking for—it will be more useful for you (and easier for them to write it) if you ask them to highlight a particular skill set or quality that will be important based on your goals.

Once you've completed the previous list, go back and review your profile with a critical eye. Share it with a few people you trust and get their feedback. Give it the same care you would for an important presentation. This is one of the most important pieces of your online presence.

Dive Deeper into LinkedIn

I've written a whole 40-plus-page guide (continuously updated) on how to get the most out of LinkedIn. If you'd like to really get into the details on your profile and the other topics I wish I had

---

more space for in this chapter, just scan the QR code to download Part 1 for free or visit unforgettablepresencekit.com.

How to Get Started Creating LinkedIn Content

Most clients who come to me for help with creating content on LinkedIn know how important it is to grow their career and to strengthen their brand, but struggle getting started for a number of reasons. Here is what I hear most often from clients:

- "I'm not sure what to post."
- "I don't want to sound stupid."
- "I don't want to be an influencer."
- "I don't have time to post every day."
- "I feel worried about how I'll come across to my coworkers."
- "I don't want to be *that person* who's always humble bragging."

First, I want to normalize these feelings. Even when I worked *at* LinkedIn, where my job was to create content, it would take me forever to hit that "post" button and share it with the world because of some of these concerns. I also want to dispel the belief that if you are posting content on LinkedIn that you need to identify as a content creator or an influencer. Reframe it as you sharing your insights and stories to help someone else along their professional journey. There is someone out there who needs to hear your story and message.

I'm here to help you push past any hesitations. When you can silence those doubts, you ensure you stay top-of-mind with your network. You become more confident and find your voice at work, and you stand out from the millions of people who have yet to try.

We'll walk through the "low-hanging fruit" of great content, how to overcome your hesitancy, and best practices for achieving and measuring success. Let's dive in!

What to Post

This is where a lot of people get tripped up. They think they have to have unique insights or groundbreaking ideas. There's advice out there that says you have to know your exact audience and create a marketing plan before getting started. I wholeheartedly disagree with all of this!

Especially when you're starting out, look around at what content is working and see what resonates with you.

"My one tip is to be a user of social media," says Natalie Marshall, the popular content creator known as Corporate Natalie. "See what's being posted. See how people are posting. There's no shame in copying the style of someone you like."

There will always be someone on LinkedIn posting similar content as you. I talk about topics like presence, introversion, communication, and public speaking, and there are countless experts out there speaking on the same topics. However, where each of us will be different is in our experiences, our stories, and simply who we are as people. If we can bring our authentic selves to our content, that is what people will resonate with first and foremost.

"I never sought out to be an influencer or a content creator or even a thought leader. I made this post about remote work. It was a Sunday night and I was in bed and just typed it out on my phone," says Jess Ramos, a senior data analyst in tech and founder of Big Data Energy Analytics. "The next morning it had hundreds of likes, and I thought, 'Oh that's kind of weird.' Later that day LinkedIn commented on my post, and it just blew up from there. That was the first time I got plugged into the LinkedIn community, and I met so many people."

Start small, and evolve as you gain confidence along the way. Trying to do too much at once can be a quick recipe for burnout when it comes to social media, so I like to break it up into more manageable steps.

Here are a few easy ideas for how to start:

- **Share:** Share an article you found interesting. If you feel comfortable, either copy and paste an excerpt or write a couple of sentences that tell people what was interesting about it for you.

- **Comment:** Commenting on other people's posts often feels less intimidating, and it's still a way for you to contribute and share your expertise. As I always like to say, comments equal content. Try to make your comments long enough that you're adding value (I typically suggest at least 15 words). Avoid comments like "I agree!" or "+1" that don't move the conversation forward. Instead, ask questions or share additional insights from your experiences.

- **Build a habit:** Try to build a habit by writing a post or creating a video. Find a cadence that feels manageable to you to start

(Is it once a month? That's fine! Is it five times per week? That might lead to burnout if you're just starting out). Try one of the three common post types: educational (let me demonstrate my expertise by teaching you something), professional (give your take on a topic trending in your field), or personal (share personal stories, reflections, and challenges you've overcome)— and don't be afraid to mix and match. Once you've created your post, ask a friend or trusted colleague to review it. Sometimes all you need is that second pair of eyes to get that needed boost of confidence to hit "post" (for me, it was my sister— thanks, Justine!).

Hook Your Audience with a Great Opening

A crucial component of any successful content, on LinkedIn or otherwise, is grabbing people's attention right away. That's why your opening (also known as a "hook") should include a surprising point of view, a vulnerable story, or a valuable takeaway.

For 50+ hooks you can use, visit unforgettablepresencekit.com.

Gain Confidence

After I left LinkedIn I stopped posting for a while—my content had been so tied to the company that I didn't really know what made sense for me to talk about (if I had been more intentional about my career brand back then, I wouldn't have run into this issue!).

A year into my next role, I started posting again because I wanted to let people know about the webinars I was speaking at. The visibility on LinkedIn led to more invitations to speak, and it created a "flywheel effect." As I continued posting, my confidence grew, and I began posting about other topics I was passionate and knowledgeable about to ensure my content wasn't always self-promotional.

While speaking gave me a reason to post, there are many other valid reasons to share your insights. For Jean Kang, a founder and content creator, it was the chance to share her passion for her field.

"I noticed that there wasn't a lot of content in program management. [Having a] greater purpose, because I was trying to help people, got me out of my shell."

Crucially, she didn't see her lack of experience on LinkedIn as a barrier. "You don't need to be a thought leader to have a story, right? Everyone has their lived experiences. Your voice matters because, if your story can help someone else with their career or their life, that makes the effort worth it."

Things to Avoid Saying on LinkedIn

As much as I love LinkedIn and think it's incredibly valuable for building your presence, it's also true that sometimes it can be overly self-promotional. There are plenty of memes and jokes on the Internet about how prevalent the "humble brag" is on LinkedIn.

People who think the site is only a place to boast about their accomplishments or sell a service or offering won't succeed long-term because they don't know how to offer value to their audience and build trust.

There's also the danger of people tuning out if something is too cliché. Instead, aim to be original and sincere. Here are a few common announcements we see on the platform and how to reframe them so you're providing value while allowing others to learn more about you:

Before	After
"I'm honored to be recognized…"	"As a leader, advocating for your teams is one of the most important things you can do. Thank you to [NAME] for being my advocate and nominating me. I'm really excited to share that I've been recognized as…"
"I'm excited to announce my new role at [COMPANY]."	"After I got laid off, it was tough staying upbeat and optimistic. I made many final round interviews but never got the offer. Now I realize that XYZ Company was waiting for me! I'm so excited to join XYZ Company as a [ROLE], where I'll get to do [RESPONSIBILITIES] and lead a team of [#]."
"I'm humbled to be invited to speak…"	"As anyone who knows me would tell you, I'm super passionate about [TOPIC]. Lately I've been diving really deep on the subject, and I can't wait to share what I've learned as a keynote speaker at [EVENT] in front of [#] people!"

The Boring Magic of Consistency

To succeed on LinkedIn, you have to give yourself the chance. Don't get in your own way by not even trying because you're worried about a less-than-ideal outcome.

Your posts may not gain much traction at first. Or even for a longer period of time. But do not give up!

Consistency is the hardest part, but if you can stick with it, posting regularly will differentiate you from the 99% of people out there.

"One of the problems that happens is that people give up really quickly," says entrepreneur and content creator Ross Pomerantz (better known as Corporate Bro). If you're not doing something consistently, then nobody's going to think of it as a thing that they want to come back for."

Pomerantz adds, "People come to me all the time. They're like, 'Hey, can you interact with us? Can you blow me up?' I'm like, do it for six months. If you create content for six months and you create even a post a week, then perhaps I'll do something. I've never had someone come back to me."

It's important to understand that almost no one builds a following overnight and you have to keep your long-term goals in mind. "You're not going to see a huge jump in followers or engagement," says Kang. "The reason I kept going was the type of feedback that I get—when people DM [direct message] me with a story that really resonates, it keeps me going and makes me feel fulfilled."

Here are the 4Es that you can follow on your content journey:

Stage 1: Explore (Posts 1–30)

- **Goal:** Get comfortable with the platform and the process of posting.

- **Action:** Experiment with different types of content (text, images, videos) without worrying too much about the perfect post. The key is to explore various styles and practice getting comfortable with creating content and hitting "post."

Stage 2: Establish (Posts 31–60)

- **Goal:** Develop a consistent posting routine.
- **Action:** Focus on establishing a habit by choosing a few core topics or themes that resonate with your expertise and interests. Aim to post regularly (e.g., a few times a week). This stage is about consistency and building a routine.

Stage 3: Envision (Posts 61–99)

- **Goal:** Align your content with your broader goals and start strategizing about the future.
- **Action:** Start to refine your content strategy by analyzing trends and data from your previous posts. Think about what type of content you want to continue sharing to achieve specific goals (increasing followers, driving profile views, generating engagement). Pay attention to which posts perform best and adjust your strategy accordingly.

Stage 4: Excel (Posts 100+)

- **Goal:** Maximize impact and engagement.
- **Action:** With a solid foundation and understanding of what works, this is where you start developing more of your voice, getting comfortable sharing more personal stories, and start meeting new and interesting folks on the platform now that they've seen your content on a regular basis.

Don't Sweat the Algorithm

I get a lot of questions from people who want to "go viral" or somehow game the algorithm into making their content soar.

The truth is that how the algorithm ranks content is constantly changing. If you want to get into the weeds, the official LinkedIn blog has an interview called "Mythbusting the feed: How the algorithm works." And, as I always like to say, an algorithm's job is to inherently learn and change.

"What I always remind people is that any algorithm, whether it's our algorithm or somewhere else, works by what people like and engage with," says Andrew Seaman, LinkedIn editor for job searches and careers. "I wouldn't worry too much about the algorithm other than just being genuine. It really comes down to, 'Is my post going to resonate with the people that I want?' If you think the answer is yes, then post it."

Measure What Matters

It's important to create great content, but how do you know if it's doing what you want?

One area I see a lot of people struggle with is measuring the right thing. They may know what their career goal is (maybe to become a thought leader or find more customers), but they don't know how to tell if they're moving closer to that goal or not. Too often they're judging success by how much content they create or by more superficial engagement metrics, rather than by what's truly important.

"There's too much emphasis on going viral. That has its place, but ultimately you're really impacting the relationships that you already have and moving them forward," says marketing consultant and career coach Brian Honigman. "I wouldn't over-optimize on getting enough post views or comments. It's more about having meaningful interactions with the people we already know, or new people reaching out to you to have a coffee conversation, inquire about a job opening, or invite you to speak at an event. Maybe a colleague says, 'Oh, I love that article you shared.' So consider how you're positively impacting your relationships in real life. Are the right people seeing my posts?"

Like Brian says, what you measure will vary depending on your goals, but here are four metrics that I think are often more meaningful than how many impressions your content gets:

- **Profile views:** This is a great measure of how interested people are in *you*. This gets measured by them actively clicking through to your profile. It's a strong signal that whatever you put out into the world was enticing enough that they clicked through to learn more about you.

- **Message and follower counts:** If someone feels moved to contact you based on something you posted, that's a clear win. A more subtle measurement is follower count. If someone decides to follow you, that tells you that they find your content valuable and want more of it.

- **Your inner circle:** It's always good to check in with mentors, close colleagues, or anyone else who's paying attention to your career. How do they feel about what you're posting? This qualitative feedback can sometimes yield insights that will never come through in quantitative stats. I've consulted with C-suite and executive leaders at Fortune 500 companies on their LinkedIn strategies; when they tell me their network shares that they're noticing and enjoying the content they post, that's a win!

- **Your return on investment (ROI):** Essentially, this is asking how much time you're investing to meet your goals. If you're spending hours every week on LinkedIn and it's getting you only a little bit closer to your goals, is that a good use of your time? Knowing your goal is so important here: things like visibility, meaningful connections, or new opportunities are harder to track, but if your effort is not yielding the rewards that you hoped for, it's a good signal to revisit your strategy. Also recognize that there may be quite a few "quiet lurkers" out there who don't show up in your metrics—just because you can't measure it doesn't mean that people aren't seeing and enjoying what you post. I've had people who haven't spoken to me or engaged with my content for years pop up in my inbox to tell me they've been enjoying my posts!

The important thing is to remember why you're putting all of this effort into content creation in the first place. Getting the results you want is the best source of energy to keep posting.

Authentic Ways to Expand Your Network

Some of you may remember a game called "Six Degrees of Kevin Bacon." In the game, you try to connect a random actor to another actor in a film they both appeared in and then connect the second (or third or fourth) actor to a movie in which they appeared with popular actor Kevin Bacon. The trick is to see who can create the shortest chain of connections to Kevin Bacon.

The game was based on the idea that anyone on Earth can be connected to anyone else by six or fewer social connections. While this is more urban myth than science, I firmly believe that this is true on LinkedIn. I feel like I can connect with almost anyone on LinkedIn using a chain of second-degree connections.

This isn't just wishful thinking on my part. It really just takes a few simple techniques to confidently reach out to people you want to connect with and have a good chance that they'll accept. I've built hundreds of relationships this way, and it's always felt aligned with who I am and what I'm trying to do.

A strong, engaged network will help you whether you're an entrepreneur or someone who wants to learn from people outside of your organization. Your network will grow organically over time if you're creating thoughtful and authentic content, as people will be curious to learn more about you (and sometimes, they may even feel like they're meeting a celebrity if you post enough!). But to really foster specific relationships, you have to do more than hope people will reach out.

How to Connect with Strangers

It's natural to feel timid about reaching out to someone on LinkedIn whom you don't know. We all get messages from people who are trying to sell us things (also known as a "pitch slap"), and it's easy to think a stranger will think we're doing the same thing.

The key is *how* you make your introduction. It's great if the person is a second-degree connection and you can have your mutual contact do the introduction on your behalf—that gives you instant credibility. But it's also not necessary. For someone to engage with you, you need to create a personalized message that tells them why you want to connect.

After you hit that Connect button, you'll be given the option to add a personalized note. If you don't include a note, you're missing out on providing important context and differentiating yourself from the sea of requests that that person may be receiving.

Your note should cover what prompted your interest—maybe it was a specific post they just shared, you know a few people in

59

common, or you just feel like you could learn from them. Don't be afraid to say what you appreciate about them. It's good to make people feel special and believe that this will be a fruitful connection.

Here are a few templates my clients and I have used successfully:

- Hi [NAME]. I'm a [TITLE] at [COMPANY AND BRIEF DESCRIPTION OF YOUR WORK]. I've been following your content and have found it really valuable as I look to grow my expertise on [TOPIC]. I'd love to connect with you.

- Hi [NAME]. Your recent post about [TOPIC] caught my eye. As a [ROLE] who [BRIEF DESCRIPTION OF YOUR WORK], I'm also really passionate about this space and would love to connect and share ideas if you're open to it.

- Hi [NAME]. I noticed we have a few connections in common. I post often about [TOPIC] and would love to connect, follow each other's work, and see how we may be able to support one another in the future.

Templates like these (combined with a strong LinkedIn presence) have helped me achieve more than a 50% acceptance rate on my connection requests—and I've reached out to as many as 200 people per week! I believe a big reason why is because the notes were thoughtful and my profile and presence were strong. With a great note but a lousy presence, your request likely won't be accepted.

If you're still feeling awkward about reaching out, try commenting on a few of their posts first. This makes it more likely that they'll recognize your name and be open to connecting (this has certainly been the case with me when others send me a request).

Want some practice? Send me a connection request on LinkedIn letting me know who you are and that you're completing this activity from my book. I'll be sure to accept! (Don't forget to add a note along with the connection request before you hit Send!)

Make a Second-Degree Connection

Just like posting, the more you get over your initial hesitation about reaching out to strangers, the easier it will become. Make a list of 5–10 people you'd like to be connected with and try out one of these templates.

Commit to doing at least one outreach like this per week (or day, or month). You'll soon find that your network is growing quickly and your LinkedIn experience will become richer. The worst that can happen is they reject the request or don't check it—and if that ends up being the case, they're missing out!

Nurturing Connections

Creating all these great new relationships and not following up on them would be a terrible waste—yet sadly it's the norm.

Aim to check in with your new or most important connections every few months. It can be a simple update: perhaps you've implemented a tip they shared on LinkedIn or you learned something recently that you thought might be useful to them.

You can even be more structured about it, like content creator and advisor Natalie Marshall (better known as Corporate Natalie). She created a networking tracker to make sure she keeps up the relationships that are important to her. "It helps me see, 'Oh, I haven't reached out to this person in a while, let's just see how they're doing,'" says Marshall. "Keeping up relationships that matter to you isn't cringy. I think it's great to say 'How's everything going? Is there anything I can do to support you?' It's very valuable."

Some people may worry that doing this in an organized way is somehow inauthentic. I would argue that just like setting aside time for your friends and family, you have to create time to nurture your professional relationships. There's nothing inauthentic about doing a good job at keeping in touch.

A LinkedIn Challenge

Are you ready to write your first LinkedIn post? Share your thoughts on *Unforgettable Presence*! (And please take any of the following suggestions verbatim.)

Step 1: Start with a hook.
Examples:

- "My 3 favorite takeaways from *Unforgettable Presence*:"
- "I just discovered a new way to level up my professional presence:"
- "These are the three transformational career lessons I'm applying from *Unforgettable Presence*:"
- "I just finished reading *Unforgettable Presence* and loved these three takeaways for how to work smarter, not harder:"
- "These lessons from *Unforgettable Presence* are ones I wish I knew earlier on in my career to be seen as a leader."

Step 2: Add additional content and personal insight.
Examples:

- I picked up this book to learn _____. It's a skill I've wanted to learn as a _____.
- Takeaway #1: _____

Takeaway #2: _____
Takeaway #3: _____

Step 3: Add a question to invite engagement.
Examples:

- Which tip resonates with you? Fellow readers: Did you have a favorite takeaway?

Bonus: Add an image of you holding the book (posts with images get double the comments[4]). If you use the hashtag #Unforgettable PresenceChallenge, I'll be sure to engage with your post!

Discussion Questions

1. What parts of your story do you want to highlight in the About section?

2. What will your first posts be about?

3. Whose content do you like on LinkedIn, and what do you like about it?

4. What are the most important metrics for measuring your success?

5. Who do you want to connect with?

6. What are your most important professional relationships that you want to nurture?

Part II

Today's Key Skills

Chapter 4

Becoming A Confident Communicator

I first learned about the power of public speaking in elementary school. I was a shy, quiet girl who did *not* like to be in the spotlight. One day, after I gave a presentation for a student showcase, my parents and I were approached by one of my friend's parents. "Wow, Lorraine did a great job! I wasn't expecting that because she's so shy." That moment opened my eyes to how being a strong public speaker could impress others and shift their perception of me, but I still avoided it at all costs.

In an ironic twist of fate, I ended up working at two major presentation companies—SlideShare (a LinkedIn company at the time) and Prezi. I learned everything that went into engaging, informative, and eye-catching slides, as well as what it took to deliver them well. I worked with renowned keynote speakers and presentation experts and soaked up what I could behind the scenes.

It wasn't until a year into my role at Prezi that I began to think about intentionally growing my own public speaking skills to strengthen my presence. I had seen over my career that those who could speak well appeared smarter, more articulate, confident, and competent. They advanced the fastest because they were so visible. As part of my commitment to becoming the CEO of my own career and being intentional, I decided to practice this skill—even if it scared me (a lot).

Communication, whether you're speaking or writing, is a foundational skill in business and a major part of presence. Being able to improve your writing skills and public speaking ability even a little bit can have a significant impact on how others see you. Being an effective communicator will help your ideas shine through, cutting through the digital noise of all the emails, chats, and presentations that we process every day. It's a skill that pays constant dividends, and there are a lot of straightforward things you can do to improve.

How to Improve any Kind of Communication

While there are tactics you can use for specific communication channels (which we'll talk about in a moment), improving your communication *quickly* mostly comes down to simple strategies you can use anywhere.

Take writing, for example. Who better to get writing advice from than Daniel Pink? Pink, a former speechwriter for Al Gore with five *New York Times* bestsellers to his name, explained to me how he boils it down to three simple things:

> *Put the audience first. It's unbelievable to me how many people miss this.*
>
> *The second thing is to simplify. As much as you possibly can. Most people don't simplify enough because they don't understand what they're talking about enough. If you have full mastery of your material, you can simplify to the right point.*
>
> *The other thing is that almost every piece of writing, in almost every speech that I ever encountered, could be a little shorter.*
>
> *So I think if you do those three things—put the audience first, simplify as much as you can, and make it shorter— you're going to be in darn good shape.*

This is great advice that will help any piece of writing. Let's look at a few more simple, specific tactics to boost your communication.

The Power of a Single Word

You've probably heard the slogan "words matter." What this means in a business context is that it's worth spending some time thinking about the right word to use that will avoid misunderstandings and spur people to take the action you want.

You'd be surprised how much a single word can influence people's behavior. In 1978, Harvard social psychologist Ellen Langer conducted what's become known as the "Xerox study."[1] In the study, a researcher walked over to a photocopier and said to the person in front of them, "Excuse me, I have five pages. May I use the Xerox machine?" The likelihood of that person saying yes was about 60%.

Then the researcher tried adding in the word "because": "Excuse me, I have five pages. May I use the Xerox machine **because** I'm in a rush?" The likelihood of the person saying yes jumped a huge amount, up to 94%. They even tried another variation, where they gave people a reason that wasn't particularly compelling. The researcher said, "Excuse me, I have five pages. May I use the Xerox machine because I have to make copies?" And that still resulted in 93% of people agreeing. It didn't really matter what researchers said after the word "because"—that word alone dramatically changed people's behavior since it indicated there was a reason for the request.

Try using this technique to make stronger and more convincing recommendations and requests. For example, instead of sending a message that says, "I know this is last minute, but I'd love it if you could present this to the team," you might say, "I know this is last minute, but I'd love it if you could present this to the team because you have a more thorough understanding of the strategy."

"Because" is just one example of how words drive action. Whatever you communicate, take time to evaluate if you've chosen the right word to get the action you want.

Use Phrases That Project Confidence

For many people who are shy or lack confidence, they default to using language that undermines their authority (particularly if speaking to people who are more senior). Minimizing words like "just" or using upspeak (ending a sentence with a rising inflection as if you're asking a question) makes them appear less confident and credible. They often don't even know they're doing it. If this is you, don't worry: by making a few simple changes, you can significantly affect how others perceive you.

To come across as more confident and authoritative in your communication, try using these alternatives:

Minimizing Language	Try This Instead
"Oops, my mistake!"	"Thank you for catching that and letting me know. I'll make sure it doesn't happen again."
"Does that make sense?"	"Let me know if you have any questions."
"Sorry I'm late."	"Thanks for your patience."
"I'll try to get it done next week."	"I will get this done by Tuesday."
"I feel we should…"	"My recommendation is…"

And make sure you avoid one of the biggest offenders, the word "just." Whether it's in phrases like, "I just wanted to add my two cents…" or "I just wanted to know if…," it's an unnecessary qualifier that weakens your statements.

These small adjustments make a big difference in your speech (or writing) and will instantly make you come across as more confident and competent. There are many of these seemingly innocuous phrases that hurt your presence—enough that I've compiled a cheat sheet you can use to identify and eliminate ones that you may be using.

Visit unforgettablepresencekit.com to grab my popular "Confident Communicator Cheat Sheet" or scan the QR code.

Exude Warmth and Competence

I love the research identified by Vanessa Van Edwards (founder of Science of People and a bestselling author) about how subtle changes to your tone can have a big impact on how charismatic you come across.

She shared with me a groundbreaking Princeton study that found that 82% of people's judgment of you is based on two traits: warmth and competence.[2] Warm words create an emotional connection, while language that reflects competence conveys expertise.

To add warmth, use words like "collaborate," "cheers," "excited," "together," and "happy." Sprinkle in an emoji or exclamation mark.

To sound competent, use words like "efficient," "lead," "productive," "streamline," and "knowledge." Back your points up with data and graphs.

In general, tone is a crucial part of your professional presence. What you say is always important, but so is *how* you say it. Your tone will impact how every single reader of your content *feels* about your message...and you. This is why a hurried, dashed-off email can leave people feeling like they're not important, while a thoughtful, well-crafted message tells your audience that you value their time and attention.

Write Better Emails

Studies have shown that the average office worker receives more than 100 emails per day[3] (and sends out a few dozen too). Break through the noise by writing an effective subject line that gets your email opened.

- **Frontload actions or descriptions.** Actions or descriptions help recipients prioritize their inbox. Start your subject line with an appropriate instruction: "Time-sensitive," "Urgent," "Action needed by April 3rd" or even "FYI, no action needed."

- **Be concise and direct.** You'll find that you can rephrase or eliminate sentences to make your message even clearer. If the email isn't time-sensitive, step away and revisit it later—you'll probably see more things you can remove when you come back to reread the message with fresh eyes.

- *Always* **include a subject line.** Even for a quick follow-up, including the subject line will help the recipient keep track of your email and make sure that it doesn't look like spam.

Once you've captured their attention, make sure to state your request first, before diving into why you need it. Sometimes people skim or don't read your entire email, so they miss what you've asked them to do.

Why Writing Is An Introvert's Superpower

Many introverts are amazing writers. Their patience and thoughtfulness is a strength that translates well to the precision that good writing demands. As Wes Kao (cofounder of Maven) illustrates, writing isn't easy. "When you start to write, you realize the idea that sounded good when you said it out loud doesn't actually make as much sense as you thought," says Kao. "There's very little room to hide in writing."

Here are four ways to use your writing skills to stand out at work:

- **Share post-meeting takeaways:** Extroverts are known to think out loud in meetings, whereas introverts are listening and processing. After a call, jot down your takeaways and connect the dots that others may not have seen, then share them and potential solutions with the rest of the team.

- **Take the lead on announcements:** When it's time to make an internal announcement on behalf of your team, raise your hand to take the lead. You're likely to get the work done faster than anyone else and attaching your name to the content will make you more visible.

- **Join the chat:** I have been in many meetings where I dive into the chat instead of unmuting to speak. I believe the chat often leads to more interesting and helpful conversations than what's being discussed out loud—precisely because participants get to be more thoughtful and thorough expressing their ideas.

- **Be active in text-based forums:** Send messages more frequently across Slack or Teams channels to get visibility in

(continued)

(continued)

> forums that aren't dependent on the loudest voice. You'll often reach more people this way too, including senior leaders who might not be in all of your meetings.

How to Become a Better Public Speaker

The ability to speak confidently in front of other people is a skill that virtually all successful businesspeople have. It's important whether you're giving a presentation to a few people or standing in front of an audience of hundreds at a conference. And yet, it's something so many of us avoid. (It's commonly said that public speaking is something people fear more than death.) Why? It all comes down to nerves.

Public speaking triggers what's known as the fight-flight-freeze response: unconscious, physiological changes in our bodies that happen when we perceive a threat, something that has stuck with us since our caveman days when potentially being ostracized from the group endangered our lives. In each case, the adrenaline starts pumping, your heart rate increases, and your senses sharpen. The reaction will usually last 20–30 minutes[4] unless you take active steps (like deep breathing or other relaxation techniques) to return your nervous system to normal.

Putting yourself in front of other people and demanding their attention also opens you up to judgment. *Are they getting value from what I'm saying? Have they heard this before? Am I sweating through my shirt?*

Part of the secret to being a good public speaker is embracing nerves as part of the process. How do you do that? The key is to understand that nerves are *a good thing*. For example, they help us stay alert and more present.

I love how entrepreneur and content creator Ross Pomerantz (also known as Corporate Bro) framed it in our conversation: He shared with me that nerves exist because "we have an opportunity to do something really cool and really great, and we're scared that we're not going to do that."

Fortunately, whether we capitalize on the opportunity is up to us. "The reality is there's a 5% chance you'll say the most profound sh*t ever," says Ross, who often speaks at large events like sales kickoffs. "There's a 2% chance that you bomb. That's a choice. You have to make the choice to bomb and the rest of the time people are going to listen to you."

Understanding that choice made a big difference for Tucker Bryant. Tucker left his job at Google to become a full-time poet and keynote speaker—two professions that require a ton of presence. For the first 18 months he was speaking and performing, he worried a lot about things going wrong and described himself as "a very nervous person."

"I felt like my job was to really know all the syllables and breaths perfectly and to not deviate from any course, because I was afraid of how I would look if I let any control go," Tucker shared with me.

The breakthrough for Tucker came from realizing that nothing terrible was going to happen if things didn't go exactly as planned.

"I had this misperception that a professional setting is super buttoned up, and that caused me anxiety. Leaning into being more human calmed my nerves," he says. "Also reframing the risk of things going differently from the way you planned. It's often not as negative as I believed, and sometimes it leads to good things."

There's a reason why we started this book off talking about mindset. It's needed in many tough situations and reframing nerves is the key that unlocks confident public speaking.

People are often shocked when they find out I'm an introverted public speaker. They're also shocked when I tell them I still get nervous. All these things can be true, *and* you can still be an excellent speaker. As one of my speaking mentors, Spencer Waldron, aptly puts it: "I think that there are two kinds of people in the world of public speaking—those who get nervous and those who are lying."

However, you don't have to let your nerves control you. Use them as a source of energy and focus. I know that nerves and discomfort exist because I'm pushing myself out of my comfort zone—which is where the most growth happens. Jenny Wood, founder of Google's Own Your Career program, agrees and says transformation happens simply by "trying hard stuff and not dying."

Most people never learn how to become strong speakers because it's difficult and scary (there's even a term for this fear of public speaking—glossophobia). If you can push past that discomfort and use these skills to your advantage, the possibilities are endless.

In the rest of this chapter we'll talk about the four practices to adopt that will help you manage your nerves and become a better speaker in any context. In the next chapter we'll hone in on the seven-step Presentation Attention Toolbox that will help you deliver compelling presentations every time.

Three Ways to Overcome Nerves in Under a Minute

What happens to your body when you get nervous? Some people get cold or hot. Others sweat. Others blush, or their mouths get dry. Maybe your heart starts racing. These have all happened to me at some point (and sometimes, still do!).

One of my public speaking mentors, Matt Abrahams, often talks about managing both symptoms and sources. Symptoms are what we feel physically and mentally (like the ones I shared above), while sources cause our anxiety. While many of us are all

---

too familiar with the symptoms we feel when we get nervous, digging into the sources can help you alleviate some of them.

Abrahams, author of *Think Faster, Talk Smarter* and a lecturer of strategic communication at Stanford GSB shares: "What is making you nervous? Is it that you're afraid of making a mistake? That you're afraid that you're being overly judged or evaluated?" Abrahams added that once you have a better sense of the cause, you can figure out the right solution, like reminding yourself of the value you bring or that you're there in service of the audience.

Let's look at a few strategies that can help target the sources and symptoms I see most often in my clients:

- **Practice 4-7-8 breathing:** Inhale deeply through your nose for four seconds, hold your breath for seven seconds, and then exhale from your mouth slowly for eight seconds. When you do this, you activate your parasympathetic nervous system, which tells your body that you're safe and don't need to activate your fight, flight, or freeze response.

- **Focus on your message:** Instead of thinking about what everyone will think of you, focus on the importance of your message and how it will help your audience.

- **Change your body temperature:** Hold a cold drink to cool down your body temperature, or hold a hot drink to warm yourself up. Our hands are powerful temperature regulators for our bodies.

Step 1: Prepare Before You Say a Word

Rich Mulholland is a former roadie who's been teaching people how to give better presentations for 27 years through his company Missing Link. In 2019 he gave talks in 26 countries on six continents. (He's still waiting for an invitation to Antarctica.) He shares one reason why nerves happen.

"All nerves are because we don't trust content," says Mulholland. "Most people don't get nervous to have a conversation, but with a presentation they get nervous because they wonder, 'What if the work I'm presenting isn't good enough?'"

The first step to projecting a confident presence as a public speaker is to make sure that you believe in your content. Part of that belief will come from knowing that it's well organized. These are a few straightforward practices that will cover a lot of your bases:

- **Signpost what's to come:** Give your audience a good map of where you're going to take them. Start by saying what you're going to talk about (and for how long); then talk about it; and finally repeat it or recap at the end to make sure everyone understands. It's much easier for your audience to follow along and focus if they know what lies ahead.

- **Create a structure:** The order in which you say things will impact the flow and whether your audience can follow along. Organize your points in a logical order. Then group them to make them easier to remember. People remember things most easily in groups of three.

- **Use stories:** People love stories and remember them easily. They don't love a lengthy list of facts, so make sure you support your ideas with examples and stories that engage people's attention and help them remember your main points. Sharing a few sentences about a customer before diving into the data and numbers is going to hook your audience in better.

Step 2: Practice Makes Perfect-ish

Once you're confident in your content, the next step is to become comfortable with your delivery.

The goal of practice is not to perfectly memorize what you're saying word-for-word—if you've ever listened to someone reading their notes off a page, you know how stilted that can sound. And when you rely too much on a script and then lose your spot, it can be really tough to find it again.

Write out a script to get an overall sense of what you want to say, but don't memorize it. Practice your key points, and then speak to those points in a more conversational way.

I recommend a few habits to make sure you're ready when the moment comes:

- **60× your practice:** When you're starting out, a good rule of thumb I learned from Waldron is to practice one hour for every one minute of speaking. That means an important 20-minute presentation requires 20 hours of practice. Realistically, you may not have that kind of time and that's okay. This benchmark is meant to illustrate just how important practice is in making you feel comfortable in your delivery. Consider breaking up your presentation in sections so that you can practice one section at a time. If it starts to feel like it's becoming stale, you've probably practiced enough.

- **Record yourself:** When you record yourself, keep going even if you stumble over your words so that you get through the whole presentation. Then watch the recording for areas of improvement (more on this later in the chapter). You can also listen to your recording while doing chores or tasks to help reinforce the content.

- **Set a routine:** Pro athletes usually have a strict routine on game day because it both normalizes the experience and also cues them to be ready when they need to be. Mulholland makes all his students do this. "It's very, very important," he says. "You want to feel like it's game time every time you walk in, whether it's into a boardroom or you're presenting to three people."

What's part of your routine doesn't matter, as long as it's consistent. Many people like to listen to the same playlist of songs or visualize how the talk will go (or, if you're like Rich, you do a few handstands before walking out).

"If I do my routine, I know I'm gonna be fine," says entrepreneur and content creator Ross Pomerantz (better known as Corporate Bro), who also follows a regular routine before speaking, including eating healthy, working out earlier in the day, and staying hydrated, among other things. "Get a routine. The more you do it, the more you become used to it."

The easiest way to get comfortable is to start small. Begin by speaking in more intimate settings or with a trusted audience, like friends or family. Choose environments where you feel comfortable and gradually expand your audience as you're ready to grow your presence.

Going from ESL Speaker to Keynote Speaker

Jia Jiang came to the United States when he was 16, without knowing a word of English and with $100 in his pocket. Twenty years later he now makes his living as a keynote speaker and gave a TED Talk that has 10.5 million views.

The journey wasn't easy, but having the courage to sound different led to steady improvement. "The more I spoke, the more confidence I got. Not just from public speaking, but just talking to people," he shared with me. "I know I still speak with an accent and that's cool. That's who I am. It differentiates me." He knows that his language skills are less important than what he has to say: "People are not there to hear me speak English. They want to know who I am. They want to know what kind of value they can get from me."

Step 3: Engage with Your Audience

One of the biggest worries people have is that their audience is not interested in what they're saying. Especially when speaking in a virtual environment, it can be hard to read your audience's reactions—does that look on their face mean they're intensely interested in what you're saying or that they're reading something on another tab?

Usually, it's best to assume good intentions. Just because someone does not look like they're totally engrossed in what you're saying doesn't mean that things are going badly.

"You can look into the audience and you'll see somebody looking really serious. Your instinct as a speaker is to go, 'Hmmm, they're not very happy or maybe what I'm talking about is a load of baloney,'" says Waldron. "But then afterwards that person will come up to you and go, 'Oh my, that was amazing.' I always say there's this huge difference between what's happening in your head and what's happening in the head of the audience. They could have been thinking, 'Did I leave the kettle on this morning?' Most people are in their internal world, even if they're looking at you. So I don't read too much into what's happening on people's faces."

Of course it's best to proactively boost audience engagement so that you never have to wonder how it's going. One tried-and-true technique is known as **pattern interrupts** or **state changes.** This means grabbing people's attention by breaking the expected pattern of you speaking and your audience passively listening. Here are a few examples you can try, which also work great in meetings, too:

- Play a video or other multimedia.
- Ask everyone to brainstorm ideas and then share them in breakout rooms or small groups.
- Launch a poll or quiz to get the audience to contribute and share the results.

Keep experimenting with different pattern interrupts and see how it changes your audience's engagement.

Why No One Cares About Your Mistake

After my first-ever virtual keynote, I cautiously opened up the results of my feedback form, heart pounding. My eyes were immediately drawn to the one piece of criticism: Someone had insulted my credibility and professionalism because I started talking with my microphone on mute. It upset me at the time, but I've learned not to dwell on things. It's unrealistic to think that mistakes will never happen.

That said, knowing that you've made a mistake—even a small one—is not a fun feeling for those of us who are Type A perfectionists. Many of us high-achievers may ruminate on alternative scenarios of what could have been, a behavior that psychologists call "counterfactual thinking."

The Spotlight Effect is also something we should watch out for, says communications expert Vinh Giang.

"We all suffer from the Spotlight Effect. We think if I ask this one stupid question, they're going to think of me for the next week and how stupid I am," Vinh shared with me. "In reality, they're thinking about what they need to get for their groceries more than they are thinking about what you said."

Allowing small hiccups to only be a brief blip on the radar helps you move through your workday with more confidence. Instead of letting mistakes ruin your day, moving on also encourages you to take bigger risks and try out more creative solutions.

Comedians probably know the importance of this better than anyone. There will always be a joke that doesn't land, but you have to keep moving forward.

"Not doing well is part of the process in comedy. I don't view bombing as a bad thing, as long as you took something away from it," says stand-up comedian and TV writer Fumi Abe. "What's amazing about comedy is you can just go to another show, and if you have a great show, now you're all good mentally."

Step 4: Conduct a Post-Talk Analysis

When you're done, make sure you take a moment to feel proud of yourself and enjoy the rush of endorphins that naturally flow. After that, in the next couple of days, spend some time analyzing how things went. This will help expedite your growth and improvement the next time you have to speak.

There are three specific ways I like to break down one of my talks:

- **Watch the recording:** No one likes watching themselves back, but it's a great way to silence your inner critic. "I just think of this as watching game film," says Daniel Pink. "I think that's a really important thing to do. And it's so easy to do that now."

There have been plenty of webinars where I thought I messed up or sounded awkward at certain points. Then I'll watch it back and realize it was all in my head. We're our own harshest critics, and we're usually all doing better than we think we are.

Replay your video in three ways: a visual review (meaning sound off to focus on your body language, facial expressions, and any presentation ticks you didn't realize you had—mine used to be rocking side to side while standing), an auditory review (to focus on how you sound, including volume, pitch, pace, and pauses), and then a holistic review, where you watch it all together.

- **Get feedback from your mentor:** We're going to talk a lot more about mentors in Chapter 8, but public speaking is a fantastic area to leverage your mentors to get feedback. I owe much of my success as a speaker to people who were willing to review recordings I sent them and give me their honest assessment.

- **Review audience feedback:** Get feedback whenever you can. Feedback from strangers can sometimes feel very direct, but it's the best way to learn. Keep the survey short but make it as specific as possible. Ask about what people thought about the content, the delivery, and what they learned. This granular feedback is a lot more valuable than a simple star rating.

Discussion Questions

1. What phrases can I remove from my writing to sound more confident?

2. As an introvert, how can I be more strategic with my communication to increase my visibility?

3. What tactic will I use the next time I get nervous before public speaking?

4. How will I improve my practice habits before my next talk or presentation?

5. What kind of pattern interrupts will I use in my next talk or presentation?

Chapter 5

Supercharging Your Virtual Presentations

In 2004, a study from Dr. Gloria Mark showed that the average person could look at a screen for two-and-a-half minutes. Today? That time has shrunk to 47 seconds, nearly a 70% decline.[1] This has huge implications for presentations.

You now have to consciously work to hold people's attention—and because many people assume that presentations will be boring and bad, audiences are quick to tune out. It's a challenge, but this also means you have a massive opportunity to shine if you do even a bit more than the bare minimum (and I know you plan to do more than that!).

"The acceptable standard for presentations is low, and often delivering a bad presentation is actually business as usual," points out keynote speaker Rich Mulholland. "People walk into presentations expecting them to be bad, so a nice presentation is actually a surprise. There's no other area of business in which we would accept that."

What holds people's attention has changed radically since work moved online in 2020. The tools have evolved, and video has become a constant part of people's lives. Outside of work people are streaming shows, watching YouTube, or cycling through videos on Instagram. Our brains now expect video to be instantly engaging and interesting, or else we move on.

This is why you have to approach virtual presentations very differently than an in-person one. Virtual doesn't have to be the less compelling option. While the content is very similar with both types, the virtual delivery has to be designed as an *experience*. As you'll see, it needs to take into account the limitations of a small screen and the expectations of your audience.

Standout virtual presentations may be your biggest opportunity to make an unforgettable impression. Not only do they make people more receptive to your content, but they give you a reputation for quality and thoughtfulness that will extend into other aspects of your work.

If creating an experience sounds daunting, it doesn't have to be. Based on expert advice, feedback from mentors, and my own trial and error, I've developed a toolbox for my own talks and presentations that I've carefully crafted over the last few years. It contains all the building blocks of a great experience. Following these steps will put you in an elite group among your peers in a way that few other things can when building out your presence.

The Presentation Attention Toolbox

The purpose of the seven-step Presentation Attention Toolbox is to make it easy for you to build and deliver a captivating and persuasive presentation.

Some people are uncomfortable giving presentations because they don't see themselves as confident, well-spoken public speakers (at least not yet). While the four steps to improving your public speaking in the last chapter can take you a long way, the solution can often be as simple as learning to "fake it 'til you make it."

Embracing your "presenter persona"—an amplified version of yourself—can create distance from judgment or self-criticism, allowing you to fully focus on your message and the audience. For many, especially introverts, stepping into this role helps overcome the psychological barriers of self-doubt or shyness—which can free you up to tap into a more powerful and commanding presence.

"To the person who's saying I'm shy and quiet, I know there's a loud version of that person. There are certainly different versions of us that exist," says communications expert Vinh Giang. "I would always say this to my students, because that psychological block often stops them. They would say, 'But that's not me,' but I tell them, 'Well, it's not you *right now*, but it can become you in the future.' I always say, don't be so attached to who you are in the present that you're not giving the future version of you a chance."

Whether you're an introvert or not, the first step is to capture people's fleeting attention.

Hook People's Attention Right Away

Your opening really sets the tone. You probably have anywhere from a few seconds to two minutes before someone decides, "Okay, I'm going to keep watching."

In Chapter 3, I mentioned the importance of a great "hook" to grab people's attention on LinkedIn. The same is true for a presentation, and while there are many effective techniques for doing this, I recommend trying one of these three:

- **Begin at the end:** Ask people to imagine a scenario in the future that gets them really excited and invested in what you're about to talk about. For example, I've used the line "Imagine a world where people walk away from your presentation feeling energized and inspired." That puts the audience in a positive mindset, and it sets the tone for what the session is going to be about.

- **Get people involved early:** You can snap people out of assuming your session will be passive by asking them to contribute early on. Ask them a question that makes them think so they'll immediately be engaged: "Did you know about...?" or "What do you think about...?" or "Have you ever thought about what it would be like to...?" This technique is especially useful for webinars where the audience gives you less time to hook them before they tune out.

- **Shock them:** Stating an unusual or surprising statement can be an excellent strategy for capturing attention.

Understand Your Audience

You can't create engaging presentation content without understanding your audience.

In his book *The Presentation*, Professor Andrew Abella recommends creating a 2×2 matrix called "From-to, Think-do" that maps out what your audience is thinking and doing before your presentation and what you want them to think and do after it. Speaker coach Spencer Waldron added "feel" as a third category to emphasize the emotional side of presentations because you often need to tap into people's emotions to get them to change. And presto, the think-do-feel matrix was born.

The matrix forces you to understand two crucial things that will help you shape your content—the current state of your audience and how you want them to change.

Let's do an example together. Start by filling out the left side of the "Think, Do, Feel" matrix for a presentation on how to lead better meetings.

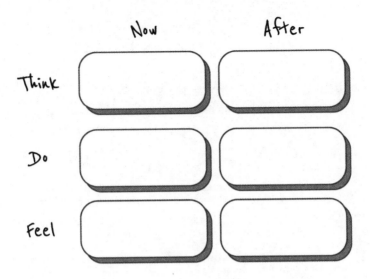

Here's one possibility of what that might look like:

- **Think:** Video meetings are necessary evils.
- **Do:** I sit down and screenshare.
- **Feel:** I'm so nervous to be on camera.

Now write down what you want your audience to think, do, and feel *after* your presentation is done.

Using this example, it might look like this:

- **Think:** Meetings don't have to be boring.
- **Do:** I use hand gestures and unique visuals.
- **Feel:** I'm excited for my next presentation!

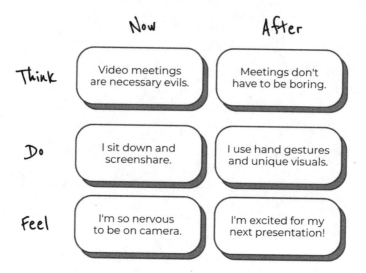

By taking the time to understand the challenges and hopes of your audience and to clearly formulate how you can address those challenges, you'll be able to make the content as helpful and interesting as possible for them.

Keep It Moving!

The more slides you have, the better.

You read that right.

We have to work harder to capture people's attention when presenting virtually. When you're talking about the same slide for even five minutes, it's an instant cue to zone out. But if you can add movement throughout your presentation—including advancing your slides—each movement is going to give a dopamine boost to the brain and encourage your audience to refocus. It's similar to why we binge Netflix and videos on social media. It's the movement that draws us in.

How much is too much? I recommend **at least two movements per minute**. Movement doesn't necessarily mean a whole new slide (although it can). These are some other examples of movement:

- Fade-in/out animations

- Videos

- GIFs

- Stickers

- Slide transitions

Whatever technique you use, don't keep your slides static for too long. By changing up what the audience is seeing, you'll help them maintain focus. Think of every movement as a trigger for someone to re-engage.

Use Arresting Visuals

Did you know that nearly two-thirds of people are visual learners?[2] This means it's crucial for your presentation to tell a visual story that reinforces your message.

Strong visuals are a major differentiator because our brains are extremely good at processing large amounts of visual information quickly and because we also remember images more easily. This means strong visuals are the quickest way to make your presentation more effective because people will retain these images (and the story they tell) better than text.

This doesn't mean your presentation should be a series of beautiful, abstract images. Each should be carefully selected to make the ideas they represent more vivid. For example, what's better: a bunch of bullet points describing the results of a study or photos of participants performing the activity being described?

When my client Melody reached out to me to help her conceptualize a presentation for an external speaking event on behalf of her company, she was experiencing what I've seen many others go through: she had become so "stuck" in a traditional old-school style of presentations (think lots of bullets and zero aesthetic) that she had trouble remembering what a captivating presentation could even look like. With just a few simple tweaks (like fading in text, substituting icons for bullets, and adding more photos), her presentation instantly looked 10× better.

There are several different approaches that can powerfully communicate meaning and improve how memorable and engaging your presentation is for people.

For example, in one of my sessions where I talk about the importance of priming, I discuss the "yogurt study,"[3] where researchers asked participants to eat chocolate yogurt in a dark room. The catch was that they were told they were eating strawberry yogurt, and as a result, 59% of them said it had a "nice strawberry flavor."

Instead of adding bullets with percentages, I added a cutout of strawberry yogurt on a spoon and then had a fade-in animation of that cutout becoming chocolate yogurt on a spoon. It was a simple visual that I'm certain my audience remembers more than text!

Slide 1:

Slide 2:

A slide with just a few words can be scanned quickly like an image. It's a great technique for communicating a call-to-action or a sound bite that you want your audience to remember. The poet and speaker Tucker Bryant relies on charged, efficient language—a few words that pack a punch—to create a vivid image. As he puts it, "One or two powerful words can bring pain or possibility to life."

As important as the visuals are, don't get so caught up in designing them that you forget your main message. "All the wonderful tools available today make it easier to create beautiful slide content. People think that you can fix a presentation with good slides," says Rich. "You have to fix the problem at the source."

Strong visuals should augment your message, not distract from it. Before you present, examine each slide to make sure it's emphasizing your point and making your message clearer. Let's take a look at this overwhelming, text-heavy slide and transform it with a few simple design tweaks—breaking up the information across multiple slides for better clarity, impact, and of course, more movement.

Q2 Recap

Revenue Growth:
· Total revenue: $5.2b, up 8% year-over-year (YoY)
· Strong growth driven by increased sales in North America (up 12%) and Europe (up 10%)

Profitability:
· Net income: $450 million, an increase of 6% YoY
· Operating margin improved to 18% (from 16% YoY)
· Earnings per share (EPS): $1.25, up from $1.10 YoY

Key Business Segments:
· Consumer Goods: $2.4B in revenue, 5% growth
· Enterprise Solutions: $1.8B in revenue, 12% growth
· Digital Services: $1B in revenue, 10% growth

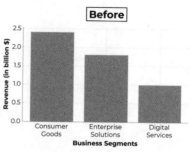

Outlook for Q3:
· Expected revenue between $5.4B and $5.6B
· Continued investment in R&D to drive innovation
· Need additional marketing head count

Q2 Financial Results

Revenue and Profitability Up (driven by NAMER)

After

$5.2B ▲

Total Revenue
(+8% year-over-year)

Strong growth driven by increased sales in North America (up 12%) and Europe (up 10%)

$450M ▲

Net Income
(+6% year-over-year)

Operating margin improved to 18% (from 16% YoY)

$1.25 ▲

Earnings per share
(Up from $1.10 last year)

Consumer goods reaches $2.4B

After

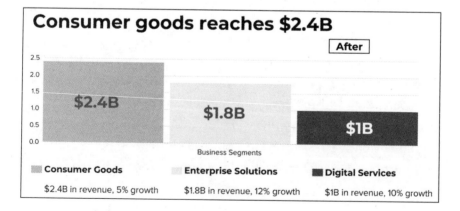

Consumer Goods	Enterprise Solutions	Digital Services
$2.4B in revenue, 5% growth	$1.8B in revenue, 12% growth	$1B in revenue, 10% growth

Unforgettable Presence

Outlook for Q3

Continued
investment in
R&D to drive
innovation

$5.4B

Expected
revenue

Request for additional
headcount to drive
marketing campaigns

Simple Rules for Good Slide Design

Strong visuals are not the only thing you need for powerful slides. Knowing the basics of good slide design is important for keeping the audience focused on your message. Finding a good template helps with the visual style, but you still need each slide to be simple and clear in its message. Here are some basics to keep in mind:

- **Go big:** Using a large font size makes things easy to read for all those people watching on laptops or phones. Too often people try to cram in a lot of text, which forces them to set the fonts at an unreadable size. Edit your text to as few words as possible, using clear fonts, so that everyone can see.

- **Keep it simple:** Do your slides pass the "at-a-glance" test? People should be able to understand the message of your slide by looking at it *without reading*. People can't read and listen at the same time, so if they have to read, then they're not listening to what you're saying.

(continued)

(continued)

- **Don't make it a rainbow:** Stick to two or three colors, ideally ones that go well with your template. The colors should help to convey your message—don't use hot pink for a presentation about an underwhelming sales report.

- **Guide the viewer's eye:** Create a visual hierarchy with the most important information first. Use size and color to direct people's attention.

Vary Your Voice

One of the biggest challenges with virtual presentations is translating your energy to the screen. You have to work a little harder for that energy to be communicated than you do in person. Fortunately, everyone has access to a good presenter's secret weapon: your voice.

Varying how you speak is a key technique for holding people's attention. Skilled presenters know how to modulate their voice in ways that grab people's attention, build interest, and signal what's important. Try these four techniques to boost your audience's engagement:

- **Add inflection:** Inflection is when you change the pitch of your voice. For example, when you ask a question, you raise your voice at the end of a sentence. Manipulating your inflection (using "all the keys of your instrument," as Vinh describes it) helps you avoid becoming too monotone and tells the audience what to feel about something: think of the different ways you can say "I'm fine" and how each one communicates its own meaning.

- **Change your pacing:** You can speed up or slow down how quickly you talk. If you speed up, you may convey that you're excited or that there's a sense of urgency. If you slow down, you may come across as more contemplative, downbeat, or serious.

- **Adjust the volume:** Speaking more loudly or softly creates different effects. If you speak louder, you can highlight key points or portray more confidence. And if you speak more softly, you will communicate more vulnerability and draw your audience in.

- **Pause for a moment:** Sometimes not saying anything tells a story too. Pausing at a moment you want to emphasize conveys your confidence and grabs your audience's attention. It can also create suspense or anticipation or signal to your audience you're about to say something important.

Raise Your Voice to Avoid Filler Words

Few things negatively impact our presence faster than filler words. Filler words are distracting to others and they make us sound less confident and prepared. A simple tip I learned from Waldron is to speak 25% *louder* than you normally would when giving a presentation.

Speaking louder naturally eliminates filler words, like "um" and "like," which sneak in when we're in a more relaxed state. That added energy requires us to be more intentional when we speak.

Try It: Pay close attention when you speak later today and observe how filler words pop up when you're talking in a more relaxed way.

Communicate with Your Body

Many people spend hours honing the message of their presentation but spend almost no time thinking about the story that their body language tells the audience. People are strongly attuned to these signals, so delivering a presentation with low energy, a timid voice, or a slumping posture tells people that you don't really believe in what you're saying. In other words, it's not just what you say but how you say it that's important.

Pay attention to where you're struggling with body language when you watch recordings of yourself and run through this checklist as a reminder before you present:

- **Keep a strong posture:** If you're able to, stand up to deliver your presentation, as you'll give off more energy and make it easier for people to focus on you. If you choose to sit, make sure you're doing so with straight posture. **Pro tip:** Scoot forward and sit on the front half of your chair to avoid any temptation to slump or lean back.

- **Breathe from your diaphragm:** Many of us have gotten lazy when we breathe, which manifests itself as breathing too high up in our chest. By "belly breathing" so that your oblique muscles expand instead of your chest, you're going to bring more oxygen into your lungs, slow your heart rate down, and have a richer tone.[4]

- **Make eye contact:** As we discussed in Chapter 2, eye contact is one of the best ways to connect with a virtual audience. Try looking into the camera or right below it (depending on your camera placement). Many of us look at the other person's face on video calls so our eyes move down, which isn't ideal.

- **Use hand gestures:** Your hands are a great communication tool. Studies have shown that showing your hands on camera makes you appear warmer, more personable and more professional.[5] To do so, raise your hands up near your chest or shoulders so that they're visible on screen. We want to avoid seeing distracting arm twitches because our hands are too low off-screen, as well as fingers popping in and out of the video frame.

- **Smile:** It sounds simple enough, but so many people have neutral or even angry expressions on camera. (Remember "resting business face" from Chapter 2?). Smiling makes a huge difference in how the audience interprets your enthusiasm and how well they connect with you. Even if you feel over the top with your energy, it's likely the perfect amount for a virtual presentation.

Finish with a Strong Conclusion

Your conclusion is a bit like the closing argument when presenting your case. You want people to come away knowing your message, understanding their next steps, and feeling motivated for action.

It's important to include the following in your work presentations:

- **A recap:** I pack a lot of information into even a 20-minute presentation. When the information is new to someone, it can be a lot to take in at once. Recaps help the information stick and remind the audience what they just learned. I continue to get feedback from corporate clients that having the recaps make a huge difference.

- **A call-to-action and next steps:** What do you want people to do? Rarely do we give a presentation just to give it. Clearly define what comes next, whether it's scheduling a follow-up call or moving ahead on a new strategy.

- **Ask for questions and feedback:** This is your chance to make sure there are no unanswered questions in the minds of your audience. Again, showing genuine interest in what people think acts as a subtle invitation for them to ask more difficult questions and can uncover obstacles that you may not have considered or addressed.

- **Invite people to connect:** If you're speaking to a new group of people, actively encourage them to connect with you. Many introverts take a while to formulate their questions and appreciate the chance to follow up with you later (especially away from the spotlight). Provide an email address or some other easy way for them to reach out. Also, if people enjoyed what you had to say, they may want to follow you on LinkedIn or learn more about your views on other topics.

Q&As and Answering Questions on the Fly

Getting asked a question we don't know the answer to can be a nerve-inducing experience. Yet it's bound to happen to us at some point (and likely many points) in our careers.

We can't control every unexpected situation that comes our way, but there are helpful frameworks that can help us think on our feet so we can respond effectively, even under pressure.

Take a look at a few common ones like: What/So What/Now What, Past/Present/Future, STAR (Situation, Task, Action, Result), or PREP (Point, Reason, Example, Point).

While answering off-the-cuff can be stressful, no one wants us to fail. Worry less about giving the perfect answer and decide which framework makes most sense in that context.

Dive into my favorite impromptu speaking frameworks at unforgettablepresencekit.com.

Discussion Questions

1. What type of opening hook will I use in my next presentation?

2. Have I assessed what I want my audience to feel and how I want them to change?

3. How can I simplify my slides? What rules of good slide design am I breaking?

4. Have I reviewed my body language while presenting so I know what to improve next time?

5. Does my presentation have all the components of a strong conclusion?

Chapter 6

Leading Meetings That Are Actually Good

When my coworker invited me to a 45-minute meeting with no agenda, I breathed out a sigh of frustration. All I had to go off of was a vague calendar title and a list of attendees. There was no Slack message giving me context, no email explaining how I was meant to contribute.

If I had to wager a guess, this is something that's happened to you, too. Unfortunately, meetings became an even bigger part of our workday when the boardroom table got replaced by a screen full of people on mute. And in this case, more certainly doesn't mean better. One recent survey[1] found that knowledge workers believe that one-third of meetings were completely unnecessary.

Many factors can create a "bad" meeting. Maybe the facilitator is not inviting you into the conversation. Maybe there's no clear agenda and everyone is talking in circles. You've been raising your hand remotely, and everyone else in person isn't noticing you. Or my favorite—the meeting that could have been an email.

This chapter won't be anything like that. Just like a good meeting should be, I'll keep it short and sweet (with information that's actually useful).

The truth is that a small set of habits and practices can make a world of difference. By learning these techniques, you'll not only enjoy your meetings a lot more, but you'll be viewed as a more competent leader and someone who knows what they're doing.

Effective meetings are one of the most important skills underlying a successful career and one of the most significant touchpoints to build your presence. They might even make your calendar a little less crowded...at least until you get that promotion.

Planning and Preparation

A meeting doesn't start once everyone enters the room. If you want to hold an impactful meeting, there's work to be done even before you send out the calendar invitation. In a hybrid office, meeting times that work across different geographies and time zones will be precious. You need to use your time well.

"The most important part of the meeting is actually the before and after of it, because it's the prep work that has gone into that meeting," says Brendan Ittelson, chief ecosystem officer at Zoom. "The person that's hosting it...do they have their materials ready? Have they actually shared some of those materials in advance so that everyone coming to the table is prepared? It's so that that time together can be the most efficient use of everyone's time for that conversation. So that prep work is huge."

Set Your Meeting Agenda

All too often, people distrust a new meeting because its purpose is vague: the organizer has a topic to discuss; they want to check in on a project; or they want to get feedback or brainstorm ideas. People think (usually correctly) that their time will not be used well.

As a meeting organizer, your job is to clearly define the goal of the meeting and list each topic that will be covered. For the goal, get as specific with it as you can. My former LinkedIn coworker Frankie always used to start off calls by saying, "This meeting will be a success if..." I loved how clear she was on why we were meeting.

It ensured everyone was on the same page and working toward a common goal.

If you want other people to contribute to the agenda, reach out as early as possible and ask them to provide topics. As the meeting organizer, it's up to you to decide if all the proposed topics should be included. Could some of them (like a project update) be better addressed with an email or an asynchronous video? Can similar topics be condensed into a single discussion point? Your job is to balance making sure that everyone has a chance to contribute with the need to protect people's time—ideally, shorter meetings are more effective and ask less of your team, so you should try to make them as concise as possible.

Once you have your agenda items ready, indicate how much time you want to spend on each one. Even better, add what you should see on the clock so people don't need to do math in their head. If your team is in different time zones, include those, too. For example:

> ≡ **9–9:05am PST/6–6:05pm CET**
> Team warm-up activity
>
> **9:05–9:10am PST/6:05–6:10am CET**
> Discuss email process changes, facilitated by Lauren
>
> **9:10–9:20am PST/6:10–6:20am CET**
> Rapid brainstorm of lead generation ideas, facilitated by Roman (make sure you have access to Figma)
>
> **9:20–9:25am PST/6:20–6:25am CET**
> Assign action items and deadlines

Finally, you need to set the length of the meeting. You'll want to stay concise, meaning that you aren't planning an hourlong meeting for the sake of it. Many fall victim to Parkinson's law, which states that work expands to fill the time you've allotted for it. Instead of defaulting to 1 hour, try a 25-minute meeting, or go even bolder and plan a 15-minute meeting.

The number of agenda items is the best measure for the correct meeting length. I recommend that agendas have no more than three discussion items for a 30-minute meeting.

Bonus points if you end your meetings five minutes ahead of the half-hour or hour. This helps your team reset and recharge so they enter their next meeting with a calm presence instead of a rushed one.

Do You Really Need That Meeting?

When I received that meeting invite from my colleague, I immediately asked to get more context on what the meeting was about and my role in it (turns out it was a brainstorm—which in corporate speak, can mean talking in circles if the facilitator doesn't have a clear plan). Once I got the context, I created a document outlining my ideas for the initiative and how I could help support it. We never had that meeting, or set up another one, because we decided to work asynchronously from my document instead.

Asynchronous communication (aka "async")—which can happen across email, collaborative documents, and even recorded videos— should be used any time real-time conversation isn't needed. For example, meetings used for simple "check-in" status updates can be done over chat. A good rule of thumb is if your meeting involves one person talking to many people or does not require immediate back-and-forth interaction, it should be async.

Replacing a meeting with asynchronous formats can lead to better outcomes by eliminating ineffective live video calls. By making these meetings async, you give your employees back time and flexibility in their schedules. They can watch videos or add comments to a document at a time that works best for them (this also ensures you get the most thoughtful ideas and responses from the introverts on your team); many videos can now be watched at 1.5× or even 2× speed and the abundance of AI notetakers makes reviewing meeting summaries even faster. There's another less spoken about benefit, too: asynchronous collaboration will also make your team happier. According to Future Forum, knowledge workers with flexibility consistently report less stress and anxiety, better work-life balance, and greater satisfaction with their jobs.[2]

Finally, a simple tip for recurring meetings that you lead: if there's nothing on the agenda 24 hours ahead of time, cancel the meeting. You'll save people logging into a meeting that they probably think is a waste of time, and you'll build trust by showing that the meetings you lead happen only when there's something to discuss.

The Perfect Meeting Invitation

You might be wondering "How hard can it be to send a good meeting invitation?" It's not difficult, but sending a meeting invitation that *contributes to your presence* is an opportunity many people miss out on.

My favorite tip is to give the meeting a name that will stand out on people's calendars. Putting some thought into what you call a meeting, and adding a bit of fun, puts people in a positive mindset from the beginning and primes them to expect something other than the same old meetings they're used to. I like to use emojis in my calendar invites, as they make the event pop on people's calendars. For example, if I'm meeting someone new, I'll use a handshake emoji and our names. You can also impact someone's perception of your meeting with words. Instead of the conventional "Brainstorm Meeting" invite, you might change it to: "Idea Power Hour."

It's a small thing, but how you show up in the details often dictates how you are seen in the big picture.

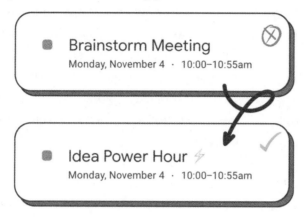

The Passive to Active Meeting Framework

The success of a meeting often comes down to one person: the facilitator. If that's you, you have a lot of responsibility on your shoulders—while it may be nerve wracking, it's also a wonderful chance for you to shine!

Meeting facilitation is more than just showing up and walking attendees through the agenda. It takes thoughtfulness and practice to do it well. Facilitators set the tone with good preparation and energy. They invite teammates into the conversation. They ask specific questions to guide the discussion. They push things toward the goal and keep the group focused on success.

I won't lie to you and say that it's easy to be a great meeting facilitator, and there's extra things to consider when it's a hybrid meeting. However, when moderation is done well, you get the chance to amplify your presence by creating a positive experience for everyone involved and showing others that you know how to lead. Enabling time to be used productively will earn you respect and create higher-performing teams. The good news is that there is an easy-to-follow road map you can follow to get quality contributions and engagement: the Passive to Active Meeting Framework.

Warm Up

A big problem with many meetings is that they start off on autopilot. People ask something like "How are you?" or "How was your weekend?" and usually get brief, tepid responses. There's awkward silence. People sit back and think it's going to be another waste-of-time meeting. Before long, participants are dialing in a few minutes late on purpose to avoid the painful ritual, which is frustrating for the people who showed up on time.

Facilitators are in many ways the new entertainers of the workplace, responsible for bringing energy and focus to the group. The first few minutes are important to get people invested. Here's a few fun questions and activities you can try:

- **Start with a creative question:** This is a fun way to learn more about your teammates. For example, ask "What Olympic sport would you play?" or "What's your favorite snack?" In my team meetings, I rotate having team members choose the question to make the success of the meeting feel like a more collaborative effort.

- **Launch a poll:** Find out the group's opinions. It could be a question related to the meeting, or what Hogwarts house they would be in.

- **Try a short group meditation:** It's great for getting everyone focused and in a similar state of mind.

- **Play a high-energy song:** This is a fun way to bring energy to the meeting right away. Create a collaborative team playlist and pick one of the songs to play each week.

Bonus Tip: Nothing induces panic and drains the energy out of a meeting faster (especially for introverts!) than asking your team to "share a fun fact" about themselves (I *still* have no idea what mine is).

Invite Participation

Actively encouraging participation is a key step to involving passive participants. I suggest three strategies to help everyone feel engaged.

Define the rules of engagement: In meetings where some teammates are in-person and some are virtual, it's much easier for people in the room to be heard than for people who are remote. Rules of engagement are guidelines that put people on equal footing so that everyone has a chance to contribute and be heard. Here are a few examples:

- If one person is remote, everyone is remote, and joins with their laptops regardless of where they are located.

- Ask everyone to use the "raise hand" feature instead of unmuting whenever a thought pops up (figuring out the exact moment to jump in is a nightmare for introverts).

- Use chat and emoji reactions. Be explicit that chat is an option, and call out the conversations you see if you're leading the meeting so contributors know they're being seen.

Address proximity bias: Proximity bias is the inherent and often unconscious tendency for humans to favor those who are physically closest to them. In the workplace, this translates into in-person workers receiving more opportunities and chances for career advancement and being viewed as more productive—just because their physical presence is felt by their bosses and company leaders.

For meeting facilitators, this means ensuring there is always a remote option. You'll also want to consider calling on remote attendees first to show that they're valued and seen, even when they're not in the same room. You can even set up your remote attendees with an in-person counterpart to help call out when they need to share something.

Encourage all kinds of participation: Once you enter the meeting, it will become your job to ensure all voices are heard, the discussion stays on track, and you end on time. While video has the ability to level the playing field, more introverted personality types may not feel as comfortable being on camera, or they may need more time to process what's being discussed.

H Walker, Vice President & Human Centered Strategies Officer at Boys & Girls Clubs of America, has made changes over the years to be thoughtful about how he leads meetings so that all voices are heard.

"Get information to people so that they can digest it and ask questions. Be open to questions, be open to ideas about changing, try different things. It's okay if everybody doesn't have airtime. If you say 'I want to hear from everybody today,' that may not be the best way," Walker shared with me.

"It may be saying two weeks in advance, 'Submit answers to these three questions. I'm open to receiving them via email. I'm open to receiving them the day of when we're in the meeting. Or if you need a little more time, I'll leave this Teams channel or chat open for three days.'"

I think the willingness to show that you will attempt multiple methods to honor everyone's style, you'll get a little bit more respect, and people may be also willing to be a little bit more uncomfortable.

Especially when brainstorming or seeking feedback, invite specific people into the conversation. If people feel like they're part of the group, they're going to be more motivated to contribute and bring their best self into the discussion.

How to Thrive in Meetings if You're an Introvert

You don't always have to be the loudest voice to make your presence known. Jean Kang, a founder and content creator who previously worked in big tech, has always felt that big meetings didn't play to her strengths. Instead, she's found her own way to contribute and ensure others see her value. "If I spot something and don't say anything, that might derail a project. [That responsibility] makes me feel empowered to share my voice," says Kang. "I think that matters because people recognize that 'Hey, Jean doesn't talk all the time. When she does talk, it's something important, so we should listen up.'"

She also recognizes that there are still opportunities to contribute even after the meeting is done. "I like to make that one-on-one connection, following up with people. After a meeting I really want to go check someone's thoughts, and I'm going to reach out to them individually or hop on another 15-minute call."

Pause and Embrace the Awkward Silence

When I began running my own meetings as a manager, one of the most difficult things I had to do was learn to embrace silence. If someone didn't speak up right away after I asked a question, I would rush onto the next thing to avoid any awkward silences.

Despite that discomfort, I know just how important it is to incorporate a "thoughtful pause." This brief moment allows everyone to process their thoughts before diving into the discussion.

Pause at least five seconds. In American culture, people start getting uncomfortable at four seconds.[3] Someone usually speaks up at second five to break that awkwardness, which triggers additional thoughts and questions from other teammates.

In a virtual and hybrid world, people don't speak up as quickly as they would in person, and they take more time to process.

Embrace that awkward silence. It gets easier over time!

Listen and Observe

Just because it's your meeting doesn't mean you have to do all the talking. In fact, you shouldn't.

Once you've got the ball rolling, you'll want to sit back and listen. Observe how others are feeling—are they leaning in and engaged or do they look like they're reading other tabs?

A virtual interface makes it easy for people to feel disconnected. A subtle but powerful technique to overcome this is to use nonverbal cues such as nodding, smiling, or raising your eyebrows to guide the conversation and make people feel more comfortable.

Move the Conversation Forward

Your job at this point is to keep things moving in a positive direction. Ask follow-up questions, build on top of what someone said, and simply thank people for chiming in. You want to create a safe space and make people feel comfortable and valued.

There are a few situations that should prompt you to jump in:

The wanderer: Sometimes the conversation starts to go in circles or drift off course.

"Someone might be blabbering on and I might say, 'That part about cost you raised brings us to the next point on the agenda.' So I interrupt, acknowledge something of significance that you said, and I move on to the next topic," suggests Matt Abrahams, lecturer on strategic communications at the Stanford Graduate School of Business. "I might even throw it to somebody else. I might say, 'Hey, that point you made about cost is really important. I wonder what Bob thinks

113

about cost.' So you see that I've not only stopped you from talking, I've said who else gets to talk next."

The monologuer: Some people just love to talk. Maybe they're excited to share, or maybe they're just missing some self-awareness—but they've started down a rabbit hole and show no sign of coming back. Raise your hand to get them to pause and get the meeting oriented back to its goal. Here's a few things you can say:

- *"I can see your passion for this subject, but we need to go back to our original topic in order to make a decision on time. Let's plan to discuss that later. Does that work for you?"* This allows you to acknowledge your colleague's excitement while getting your colleague's buy-in to focus on the task at hand.

- *"These are some great points, and I want to hear more offline since not everyone in this meeting works on that project."* Here again, you're not totally squashing your colleague, but you are pulling back to the central focus and showing respect for your colleagues' time.

- *"Thanks for sharing. We've got a full agenda, so we need to get back to [agenda item]; let's talk offline after this meeting."* Yet another reason to have a solid agenda with time limits.

The interrupter: Other people like to jump in before people have finished their thought. This can be frustrating for all involved, so you have to be proactive to get things back on track:

- Speak with confidence, and avoid minimizing phrases like, "I just want to add" or "Let me know if I'm misunderstanding, but..." Using phrases like these make it easier for others to interrupt you. Also avoid uptalk—ending each sentence with a rising inflection, like it's a question.

- To stop one colleague from interrupting another, you can jump in with something like, "Ken, I'd love to hear what you have to share, but I don't think Sonia was done with her thought."

- If this person is a serial interrupter, it's appropriate to talk to them about this issue outside the meeting. Be kind but forthright, and talk to them about how their interruptions are affecting others from participating.

An imbalance of extroverts and introverts: If you're dealing with a virtual room of extroverts, you'll be best off facilitating and making sure everyone gets a word in. If it's a room of pensive introverts, give them a heads up before asking for their input so they can have a few moments to put their thoughts together.

"If it's a free for all and everyone is just jumping in, then naturally the people who are comfortable with that format will do it more often," points out self-described introvert Dorie Clark, executive education faculty at Columbia Business School. "The format is handicapping the transmission of the best ideas. So it's the facilitator's responsibility to set parameters that enable better participation."

After the Meeting

You can have the most fruitful and productive meeting in the world, but if you aren't clear about what comes next, all that time will have been for nothing.

It's up to the facilitator, or a dedicated notetaker, to summarize the call. Write down and communicate specific deadlines and action items and then distribute them to relevant stakeholders.

Note that AI can be a great tool here. If you've recorded the call, you can share the transcript with anyone who wasn't able to attend, and most AI note-taking apps will also generate a meeting summary and action items.

Ask for Feedback

I believe that if meeting facilitators sent out feedback surveys more often, we'd improve our corporate meeting problem exponentially. After each meeting, I recommend sending a brief poll or survey to gauge a few key things:

- Was it a good use of your time?
- Was the meeting the right length?
- Was the meeting facilitated in a way that gave you a chance to contribute?

You can create variations on these questions. For example, create a scale from one to five, and if the score is any lower than five, it's a great opportunity to get more clarifying details for what would've gotten you that perfect score.

It's important when you get this feedback to act on it and show that you're listening. If attendees start seeing that their feedback is getting implemented, they'll be more likely to keep sharing and be more engaged during your future meetings.

Checking in every now and then with your team, by using the start, stop, continue method for your meetings, can be beneficial, too. Ask your team: What should we start doing? What should we stop doing? And what should we continue doing?

Lastly, when you ask for feedback, make it as specific as possible. Asking "How was the meeting?" isn't going to elicit very helpful feedback. Instead, you might ask, "As a meeting facilitator, I'm focused on finding ways to ensure everyone has a chance to contribute during meetings. On a scale of one to five, how would you rate my facilitation and did you feel like you had enough time to process the information shared and share your thoughts?"

Remember, your meetings are one of the best ways to build your presence. Many of us accept that meetings are inherently bad, so by creating a productive and engaging one, you're sure to impress your colleagues.

Download the Memorable Meeting Checklist at unforgettablepresencekit.com.

Discussion Questions

1. How can I improve my meeting agendas?

2. How can I make my meeting invitations more fun and informative?

3. What are some good icebreaker questions I can ask when facilitating a meeting?

4. How can I do a better job of encouraging participation at my next meeting?

5. What kind of feedback should I ask for after the next meeting that I facilitate?

Part III

Career Advancement

Chapter 7

Making Yourself Unforgettable
to Executives

During my junior year at university, I had the unique opportunity to shadow the president of a major movie studio for a day.

When it came time to sit down with her, her first question to me was, "What do you know about the studio?" I was embarrassed to say that I didn't know much.

It turns out that during her co-presidency, the studio received 122 Golden Globe nominations, 159 Oscar nominations, and 40 Oscars, including four Best Picture Awards.

She then shared one of the most important lessons of my career: be prepared before you meet someone.

My cheeks burned as she gave me this feedback, mortified that I'd messed up this first impression.

Few things are more impactful on your career than the impression you make on influential people. Having good relationships with executives can make or break your reputation. Usually, these impressions are formed in a very short period of time—even in as little as 1/10 of a second.[1] And it's in these fractions of a second, whether in high-pressure situations like large meetings or casual conversations at the beginning of a call, that can set you on the right path. The best way to be ready is to prepare *ahead* of that encounter.

"Know what your moments are to stand out and really invest in those moments," says keynote speaker and poet Tucker Bryant. "You may have two minutes to open up a conversation that helps executives get to know you, learn that your work is good, and develop an impression of you."

Many people overlook these moments, or feel intimidated by them, but I believe that being ready for them is a crucial part of having an unforgettable presence. If you have the chance to speak with an executive, it's a unique opportunity to be *seen* both in the right place *and* by the right person.

Leaders gravitate toward people who they like and respect. Knowing how to communicate effectively with executives is one of the quickest ways to give your career a boost. Don't waste this exciting opportunity!

Five Ways You Can Make a Strong Impression on Executives

While making a strong impression with executives is something that anyone can do, it's a lot less clear *how* you do it. Many people try to "put their best foot forward" or put on a happy face. Others give executives the equivalent of a book report on all the things they've been doing, rather than understanding what executives actually want to hear.

How to succeed comes down to understanding how an executive's needs are different from those of your manager or your coworkers. "There is a good chance that the person you're communicating with has had 40 other people communicate with them that day," says Spencer Waldron, a public speaking and presentation coach. "That means if you want to stand out, you need to start with a clear ask and then provide the context, share the key arguments, explain why they matter, offer options, and make your recommendation. Show that you've done your homework and left no stone unturned."

This is a great formula for delivering your message and impressing executives.

Let's take a look at what else you can do to shine during those important encounters.

Learn Their Communication Style

Most people have preferences around how they like to receive information (for example, in-person versus asynchronously). Executives often have unique and specific preferences that you need to know if you want your message to have maximum impact.

"You have to understand that executive and how they look and think about the world. Personally, I'm a details person. So I will go very deep and want to know a lot of details and the edge cases and nuances, but that's my style," says Brendan Ittelson, chief ecosystem officer at Zoom. "I know other executives that I work with, that's not their style. They're more big-picture, looking at the universal approach. So if you're not a match for their style, it will be a very poor conversation because you're not communicating the items that each individual needs."

The easiest way to find out is to simply ask the person about their preferences (or, if they're busy, their executive assistant will be an excellent resource). Here are some sample questions you can start with:

- Do you prefer shorter messages or detailed reports?
- How often do you like to receive updates on projects?
- Would you rather watch a video or have the information written out?
- Do you like to grab people for quick face-to-face discussions, or do you prefer discussing through chat first?
- What are your main goals and objectives? (This will allow you to tailor your messages to support those goals.)

Asking these kinds of questions is a great way to start off your relationship with any executive. It shows you are sensitive to their needs and serious about being as effective as possible for them.

Email Haiku

I love this idea that Kim Scott, author of *Radical Candor,* shared with me, which not only applies to executives but to anyone you work with.

"Email haiku is about making sure that when you're sending an email, the key point has to fit into one iPhone screen. Make it so they don't have to scroll, even with a big font. You want to make sure that you're being respectful of their time and that means summarizing the key points, it means doing some formatting if there's more stuff that needs to be said below the screen. It can take an hour to craft a one sentence email, but it's worth spending that hour, it's worth making sure that you have some compassion for the fact that the person you're emailing is busy and may not have time to open up that attachment."

Understand Their Priorities

Before you start a conversation with an executive, try to put yourself in their shoes. A common mistake that people make is that they focus so much on what they themselves want to say—their big idea, why it's so exciting, and all the reasons it should happen—that they forget what the other person needs to hear before they'll buy in.

Think about how to align your message with what the executive cares about. This is where you have to understand their interests, your organization's mission, and the company's goals. Think about (or ask someone) the key questions keeping that executive up at night and what's currently on their plate.

This often means you'll need to dive into the metrics. Read company reports and strategy documents to learn more about the business. Make sure you know not only the company's key performance indicators (KPIs) but also the specific ones that this person is being evaluated on. Once you understand their goals, it will be easier to tailor your message to them.

Finally, understand that they have a different view on the company than you do. "One mistake that people make is that they don't realize that they [direct reports] have a much narrower but deeper perspective on a situation," says Kim. "And their boss has a broader one but shallower."

To understand their perspective, ask yourself two questions:

- What do I know that this person doesn't (but should know)?
- What does this person know that I don't (but should)?

In the first example, this might mean important client feedback that the executive isn't aware of. For the second question, an example might be how work in other departments affects your project.

By understanding what's important to a company leader, you'll be able to position and share information, projects, and updates in a way that an executive will appreciate.

How to Craft a High-Impact Message

In a past role, I had to present weekly updates on social media performance. I gave all the numbers possible and went way too

(continued)

(continued)

far into the weeds. Each time it was my turn to speak, I could feel people losing focus, both through the computer screen and in the room around me. It was a data dump, when I should have been doing a curated analysis.

This type of oversharing is a common problem and has led me to develop three rules that I use to "test" my messaging before sharing it with an executive.

- **Always have an opinion or recommendation:** Executives value individuals who can express a viewpoint that's backed with data and facts. Providing your opinion or even pushing back respectfully can be a value-add, as you're often much closer to the details.

- **Avoid information overload:** When you've worked on a project, it's common to think that all information is important information. And while it may be to you, an executive only wants to know the key points. Focus only on what the executive needs to know.

- **Get off the treadmill:** The concept of treadmill and destination verbs was created by author Ann Latham. You want to replace treadmill verbs (like review, discuss, and share) with destination verbs (like decide, deliver, or confirm). The latter moves the work forward and requires action, while treadmill verbs send the conversation in circles with no clear destination.

One week I decided to change it up. I highlighted trends week-over-week and month-over-month and shared what topics resonated based on the data; I connected the dots and gave others learnings they could take away for their own work. This time, people were much more tuned in.

Master Meetings and Presentations

You've landed a meeting with an executive. While you may be having sleepless nights and nerves, I want you to reframe this as an exciting moment—because it is!

Here are six things to keep in mind for your next meeting:

Prepare them: Make sure the executive has the information they need *before* they get to your meeting. This can be as simple as sending them the agenda ahead of time or perhaps sending them materials to read beforehand. Giving an executive the information they need means you can save time presenting your findings and move quickly into getting their input on what to do.

Be explicit about the goal: Many executives are jumping from meeting to meeting, which means they are constantly switching context. You want to make it easy for them to get up to speed and remember what the end goal is.

"I want to acknowledge an executive's goals, show how we're trying to address those goals, and explain how what we're doing isn't working," says Tucker. "I want to show them I have something better to offer and what we can do if we make that shift. By the end, I want them to say that I've brought them along in a way that is emotional but also logical."

Be ready to move fast: Every second counts with an executive, given how limited their time is, so you need to be efficient. But don't fall into this common trap that Maven cofounder Wes Kao shared with me: "Being prepared to move fast doesn't mean talking really fast with a tone of anxiety and urgency," she says. "Usually the brains of senior leaders move quite quickly. They have a lot more context than you do. They're sometimes impatient. So if you have a deck with 20 slides and you can get your point across in three, take the win and move on."

Get to the point: Executives want information distilled down for them. A powerful technique is called BLUF: Bottom Line Up Front.

"It's a military concept for concise communication that I really like," says Kao. "If the person understands the main point, they don't have to read the rest of the context. Why make someone ask a billion follow-up questions to get the information they need when you could offer it voluntarily in the first place?"

One simple way to implement this approach is to add detail to your slide headers. Instead of titling a slide "Project Update," try calling it "Project Update: Requires more marketing budget for new campaign." This saves the executive the time and effort of reading the slide to find out the key takeaway. (In fact, I recommend doing this even when you're not presenting to executives!)

Always have an action item: Executives rarely come together just to receive updates or discuss things without any resolution. They're there to make decisions, remove roadblocks, and address urgent issues.

I saw this play out when I spoke to a group of culture champions who were struggling to inspire action from their executive sponsors. Often they asked for "support," but it was too vague to result in any meaningful action. I recommended they make their message to sponsors more focused and specific. Let's take a look at two possibilities:

Option 1: *"I'd love your support on this initiative."*

Option 2: *"I would love for you to send a Slack message to our team channel, and I've drafted up a message for you."*

If you were a busy executive, which one would you be more likely to take action on?

Make it clear what you need them to do. If you're not sure, then you need more research to understand what the costs are (whether in money, time, or company resources) that you need this person to approve.

Expect to get interrupted: I was a few weeks into my new role at Prezi, and one of my first assignments was presenting my team strategy to the CEO. I walked into the room with confidence, ready to take everyone through my presentation.

I probably got through three slides when the barrage of questions began.

That experience taught me that executives often ask questions during presentations, even if you mention that you'll take Q&A at the end. They usually prefer dialogue over monologue, so don't get flustered or take it personally if you're interrupted. Executives want clarity as quickly as possible. Just because they're asking a lot of questions, it doesn't mean that things are going poorly or they don't respect what you're presenting.

As you can see from my experience, while it's important to prepare for the presentation, it's just as important to prepare for the Q&A.

Here are five questions that often come up:

- **What happens if we do nothing?** This seeks to understand potential consequences and risks, as well as impact on the bottom line if no action is taken.

- **What do you need from us?** This is asking about what the next steps are if they want to move forward. Make sure you have your action plan ready.

- **Who else needs to be involved?** This is about determining which teams you'll need to work with in order to be successful. It's helpful to get their buy-in before the meeting to show that you came prepared.

- **What priorities should this project take against project X?** Everyone is busy with a different set of priorities. Make sure you understand what else is going on in the business.

- **What's your recommendation?** Make sure you have an opinion on the best path forward that's backed with facts and data.

Making Small Talk with Executives

Few things make people sweat like the idea of an awkward interaction with someone important (and it's especially true for my fellow introverts!). These encounters usually happen without warning (passing each other in the hallway or being the only two people on the call before a virtual meeting), so it's good to be ready. Done well, these little moments can help you appear comfortable and confident, while building a relationship with someone important for your career.

- **In the office:** Have a few sentences planned out describing your role and what you're working on. Anchor yourself in their minds by saying who you work with whom they also work with.

- **At social events:** Ask about their hobbies and passions outside of work and see if you can discover any shared interests. Keep your questions open-ended and share a little bit about yourself to keep the conversation flowing.

- **Quick encounters:** Ask open-ended questions like "What was the highlight of your weekend?" or offer some work-adjacent information about yourself. For example, "I listened to this podcast the other day about [TOPIC] that really made me think about [COMPANY PRIORITY]."

To make sure your responses are thoughtful, try **conversational threading:** a technique that helps keep conversations going by giving the question asker multiple "threads" to pull from.

Unforgettable Presence

Typical conversation:

- *Executive: How was your weekend?*
- *You: It was good, thanks! How was yours?*
- *Executive: Good!*

With conversational threading:

- *Executive: How was your weekend?*
- *You: It was good! I went to my niece's birthday party, and my whole family was there; then I did my usual three-mile run.*

In the previous example, you've given the executive a few threads they can pull on: They could ask about your niece, your family, or your hobby.

Build Credibility and Trust

Bestselling author and Wharton professor Adam Grant said something I love (referring to space flight): "If you look at great crews, you'll see trust at the heart of their success. If you don't trust the people on your team, you'll end up playing it too safe. Trust makes it possible to aim higher, to leap further, and to know that someone truly has your back if you fall."[2]

If you are seen as more credible and trustworthy, executives are more likely to open doors and unlock new opportunities for you. Your reputation will naturally solidify, and you will be viewed as a leader.

To build this kind of trust with leaders, there are a few essential ingredients:

Provide options: Offer up a few options and explain the pros and cons of each based on what you know is important to that person. Executives are always balancing risks and trade-offs—if they agree to your request, they may need to shift resources from another project. "Most executives care about three things," says Spencer Waldron. "Is this going to bring in revenue? Is there a risk to it? And what's the cost?" If you can provide multiple options that address these questions, this will show you're thoughtful, you did your research, and that you're open to multiple perspectives.

Be honest and transparent: Executives are good at spotting when you're holding something back or making up an answer on the spot. Be straightforward and honest about any challenges or less-than-ideal results or metrics, and come to the table with ideas for how you might improve the situation.

Part of coming across as honest is speaking confidently. If you can't deliver your message confidently, it can leave the impression that you don't believe it. Avoid using tentative language or speaking so quietly that you seem unsure of yourself.

Follow through: It's crucial that you do what you say you're going to do, when you say you're going to do it. It sounds like the most basic thing, but many people don't do it, and it's an instant trust zapper. This doesn't mean there's no room for deadlines to change—if that's the case, be proactive in letting relevant stakeholders know (and don't forget to come up with different solutions to ensure you're not slowing down the team!).

For example:

I may need to push out our deadline by three days because the client isn't providing us with the information we need. I'm giving them one more day to reply, and in the meantime I'm gathering a few testimonials from other customers to have as backup. I've also let the design team know that we will be delayed a few days and worked with them to come up with a solution so we still deliver a great product.

Bonus Tip: If things are going along as planned, don't assume that no updates are needed. An executive will appreciate the information, even if they don't always take the time to respond. No one will ever complain that you communicate too much, but not enough communication will create a lack of trust and can lead to things like micromanagement.

Get Comfortable with Numbers and Data

Executives are focused on strategic goals and metrics-driven outcomes. Data and numbers are often what they use to make decisions. It can be intimidating at first, but it really pays to learn to speak their language. That means using data in an easily digestible way when communicating. I follow three best practices to make sure I'm sharing numbers in a way that adds value:

- **Provide context:** Saying that online traffic for your company grew 30% year-over-year might sound like good news, but not if it grew 70% last year. Always provide the full picture when providing data, which includes trends, comparisons, and anomalies. Executives usually have a good grasp of the important metrics, so they'll notice if something isn't what they expected.

- **Identify what's important:** It's understandable to want to show off all the data you've collected, but that will only confuse and overwhelm your audience. Executives care only about the important data points and will appreciate you being able to sift through and pick out what they need to know. Think of yourself as someone who curates information, not someone who delivers all of it at once.

- **Make it visual:** Whether you show your data in a chart, a pie graph, or something else entirely, make sure the most important part of your data stands out. Highlight the key areas with an arrow, a circle, or shading to show your audience what to remember and reinforce your takeaways.

Four Key Metrics to Boost Your Financial Literacy

It's great to communicate numbers clearly, but it's even more important to understand what they mean. I made an effort to become financially literate later than I should have, but once I did, it allowed me to understand the health of the business and what's important to the executive team. While every business will have particular numbers that it emphasizes, understanding these four will help you in almost any situation.

- **Revenue growth:** This refers to the increase in a company's total sales over a specific period, usually measured year-over-year or quarter-over-quarter. How quickly revenue is growing often drives resource allocation, hiring decisions, and overall business strategy.
- **Profitability:** This is the difference between a company's revenues and expenses, often expressed through a metric like profit margin. A company's profitability will affect the decisions it makes about pricing, costs, and expansion.
- **Cash burn:** This is the pace at which a company is spending its cash reserves to fund operations and growth. It's particularly relevant for start-ups or companies in growth phases, as it shows how much "runway" (or time) a company has before it must become profitable and/or bring in more funding.

- **Customer retention:** This is the ability of a company to keep its customers over time. High customer retention rates often lead to increased profitability and steady revenue streams, while low rates (also called a high "churn" rate) can signal that customers are not getting the value they want from the company's products or services. Generally speaking, higher retention rates correlate with stronger, more resilient businesses.

If you're feeling overwhelmed, find someone who understands these metrics to walk you through them. One thing I found valuable in my last role was to sit down with my manager every quarter to go over the latest company financial reports to make sure I understood them.

Discussion Questions

1. Which executive's communication styles do I need to learn more about, and who can I learn this from?

2. Which company metrics do I need to learn more about to understand my executive and their priorities?

3. What can I do to better prepare for my next meeting with an executive?

4. What can I do to build my credibility with my executive team?

5. How can I improve my understanding of and present data and metrics?

Chapter 8

Building Influence at Any Level

Influence is the ability to make things happen. When you have it, it doesn't just mean that people will listen to you. It means that what you say carries weight—and can even change careers.

Soni Basi—a PhD in social psychology and former global chief people officer at Edelman—has seen this firsthand many times. But the story she shared with me about how someone else's influence changed her career really stuck with me.

> *I was presenting to a group of 200 leaders in Greece. In the audience was a chief HR officer (CHRO) and the person who became my future boss.*
>
> *After the talk, the CHRO put his arm around my shoulder and said to a colleague of his at a large pharma company, "We need to hire Soni."*
>
> *The job they wanted me to do (Global Director of Learning & Development) was new to me. Working within a company rather than as a consultant was new to me. Moving from Chicago to New Jersey would be new for my family and me.*
>
> *But I thought, "He is a seasoned CHRO, and he thinks I can do this job. So if he thinks I can do this job and he wants me to move from Chicago to New Jersey and he's willing to pay for my move, he is not going to let me fail, right?"*

That was a moment for me where I realized people will put you in the right rooms, and they will allow you to shine because it reflects well on the decision they made to hire you or promote you or bring you into that room.

They will not invite you into the rooms if they feel that you will not make them look good. And that was a game changer for me that boosted my confidence, gave me voice, and gave me agency over my career.

What's amazing about this story is not only that one person's vote of confidence opened up a new door in her career but that the same vote of confidence made her believe something new.

Throughout my career, I've seen many leaders who have influence. They're the ones always invited to important meetings, whose opinions are sought out on difficult issues, and who seem to know (and be liked by) everyone. While working in corporate, I knew I wanted to be someone like that, but I had no idea how to get there.

It wasn't just about the work—it was about how they interacted with people. Thankfully, as you've seen throughout this book, all these skills can in fact be learned. Enter the RAVE Model: an easy-to-remember acronym to give you a holistic way of thinking about influence. In this chapter, we'll look at its four major components and how you can improve in each aspect of influence-building.

We'll also look at how to develop some of the most influential relationships of your career—by finding and working with mentors and sponsors who are invested in your development and advancement.

Finally, we'll dive into the misunderstood subject of networking and why it can actually be…fun?

At the heart of building influence is developing a broad network of relationships at work. It turns out that having lots of good relationships, both inside and outside your organization, is what makes work both more satisfying and rewarding. For example, there's abundant research that says having a "best friend" at work makes you more productive, innovative, and happy.[1] It's great to flex your expertise, but it's the time spent on your relationships that have the biggest impact on your success and how much you enjoy reaching it.

Grow Your Influence with the RAVE Model

There are lots of ways to become more influential—what matters is finding the methods and tactics that work for you. To think about them systematically, I created the RAVE Model: relationships, appearance, visibility, and expertise. These are four key areas that you can develop to increase your influence, whether you're early in your career or further along, an introvert or an extrovert, virtual or in-person.

What's important is to understand what you're doing in each area. Maybe you put a lot of effort into relationships, but don't think about your visibility. Maybe you're good at demonstrating your expertise, but you don't dress for success. Analyzing how you perform in each aspect will help you uncover opportunities to increase your influence.

While there are many potential tactics, we'll look at one specific strategy in each area that you can use for quick improvements. Let's dive in!

Relationships

Ross Pomerantz, the entrepreneur and content creator known to many as Corporate Bro, sums up why workplace relationships are such a crucial part of building influence: "How are you treating everyone else? Such an important part of moving up in a company is simply how you are human with other people. If you're genuinely curious about how other people are doing, people like that. It's good for both people."

There are so many ways to build workplace relationships, some of which we've already talked about (like turning off autopilot small talk and using collaborative language) and others that we'll talk about later in the book (like how to work with your manager). But the biggest thing is making time to get to know people on a personal level. It's *so* easy to forget to do this—everyone is busy and taking a break from work to "get to know someone" can feel like a luxury you don't have. But these relationships become crucial when you need information, need to have a foundation of trust before starting a complex project, or need a colleague to support you when you're up for promotion. It also makes work a more fun place to be.

Here are a few things you can do to develop new relationships:

- **Set a goal:** You'll always be more successful if you can give yourself a tangible target. Try aiming for something like meeting one new person a week and see how your gains compound over time.

- **Join an employee resource group (ERG):** Join an ERG or committee that's not directly related to your job. This is a wonderful way to connect with people across the company you wouldn't normally encounter.

- **Be a cheerleader:** When people share updates in a channel, be quick to add an emoji or offer a positive comment. They'll appreciate you for being supportive in a public way.

- **Show vulnerability:** Offering up something about yourself tells people that you trust them, and makes them more likely to reciprocate. This is a cheat code for developing trust and the foundation for a strong relationship.

Appearances

Appearances are all about the way you appear to others: what your body language says when you're speaking or your eye contact and facial expressions on a video call. It's about appearing attentive and interested, as it's hard to influence people if they don't feel like you're tuned in with what they have to say.

What you wear is also important. You want to find the balance between what you feel good and comfortable in and how others will perceive your appearance.

Thankfully, workplace dress codes have really evolved over the past decade, and it's much more accepted to wear casual clothing that feels authentic to you. In many workplaces now, you're more likely to get compliments for your sneakers than your suit.

That said, just because you don't always need traditional work attire doesn't mean you shouldn't aim to look your best (whatever that means to you). There are two particular situations where I think you should put extra care in your appearance:

- If you're not in the office every day, then the days you are there have an outsized impact on people's impression of you. In most companies, there's a different standard for in-person meetings than virtual ones.

- When you are giving a presentation (or any other high-stakes situation) and all eyes are on you, what you wear is part of how you communicate. If you're communicating via video, aim for jewel tones to pop on camera, avoid stripes (they'll look like they're moving due to an effect called moiré), and make sure you wear a different color than your skin tone and your wallpaper.

Visibility

At the beginning of this book, I said that professional presence is made up of two factors: how and where you're seen. Visibility refers to the second part. The harsh reality is that even if you're the smartest, most productive worker in the room, it won't matter much if you're not being seen in the right places and by the right people.

"There are so many benefits to letting your colleagues know what you're working on and what you're excited and passionate about," says marketing career coach Brian Honigman. "Marketing yourself is important as a professional because you can tell people, 'Here are my accomplishments; here are the things I'm great at.' It's a way to show rather than tell."

Visibility is something I struggled with, particularly early on in my career, in part because of my cultural background and because of my naturally introverted nature. There are a couple of ways to help you become visible that I've shared with people across different company sizes and career levels.

- **Become a "bragger":** One concern I hear time and time again is that if I toot my own horn, I'm going to be that annoying person who is always talking about themselves.

This sentiment is particularly true among Asian professionals: A 2019 study by the Asia Society found that the majority of people from Asian backgrounds prefer to express themselves privately and don't like to disagree with others in public.[2]

It's all in the reframe. If you can share learnings on the job (and how others can apply them) or show progress toward your team's or organization's goals (which others benefit from), you are providing valuable information in a way that doesn't feel like you're bragging or being obnoxious.

Remember how we need to become the CEO of our own career? That means letting others know about your business—aka *you*! If not you, then who?

World Class Speakers founder and Asian American Pacific Islander (AAPI) advocate Jerry Won summarizes it best: "If it happened, it's not bragging."

- **Find the right spaces:** When I became a director, I got added to a Slack group titled #senior-leaders. I had no idea this existed! I immediately told my team about it so they knew I could help them socialize their work there.

Why? Because this is where all the senior leaders were active, including the CEO.

There were plenty of times when I'd share my wins or announcements in a small team channel. It was great that my team knew, but you have to think beyond your immediate bubble to start gaining influence within an organization.

- **Volunteer to present:** This book has a strong emphasis on speaking and presentation skills because they have so many positive impacts. It can be uncomfortable at first, but showing that you're ready for the challenge will leave a strong impression on people. Start by speaking to smaller groups and build up your confidence to an all-hands meeting—your influence and visibility will grow every time others see your face.

Expertise

Having unique expertise can really set you apart from your peers, both inside and outside your organization. But you need to demonstrate it! Building your reputation as an expert in your specialty is so much more than just doing the work.

We've talked about a number of ways to do this already—such as posting to LinkedIn and speaking regularly on a topic—but there are also some less intuitive ways you can stand out:

- **Feedback is a way to show expertise:** Helping people improve at what you're already good at is an efficient way to both build goodwill and employ your skills in a productive way. It's not about showing people that you "know the right answer," but demonstrating that you have the confidence (and kindness) to share your knowledge to help others.

- **Curating content:** You don't always have to be an expert to be seen as having expertise. When I was asked to help support the public relations team in my last role, I set up Google Alerts for relevant news topics and would often be the first to share it in our team's Slack channel. I became known as someone who stays current and has helpful information to share. If you can also pull out quotes or insights that you find interesting from the content, even better.

Grab your RAVE Influence Workbook to start building your influence at work at unforgettablepresencekit.com.

Finding Your Advocates: Sponsors and Mentors

This is one of my favorite cheat codes for growing your influence. Developing relationships with people who are a bit further ahead of you on their career journey, and having them actively support you, can pay incredible dividends.

"You have to be bold enough to pay attention to a leader that is doing great work and going after that leader and ask, 'Hey can you be my mentor?'" says Joey Aviles, a transformational keynote speaker and lead researcher. "It's critical if you are in a place where you are not being noticed."

Most people are familiar with the role of mentors but are not always clear on the difference between a mentor and a sponsor. Let's take a closer look.

Mentors are primarily concerned with your personal and professional development. They can help you over the long term with guidance and advice, sharing their expertise and industry insights. They are a bit like a coach, helping you take your game to the next level.

"There's no bigger unlock for someone's personal advancement than being mentored by a person who knows the value of connection and guidance," says Brandon Carson, a global development leader and author. "The cornerstone of effective mentoring is one-on-one conversations. I can help the mentee by guiding them through challenging situations, asking questions to get to the root of their purpose and needs, offering suggestions and feedback, sharing resources with them, and helping them problem solve."

Sponsors take a more direct role in your career advancement. They are your voice when you're not in the room and will advocate for you when opportunities come up that can benefit your career.

They're more like your champion, clearing your path and opening doors for you (like Soni Basi's sponsor did for her after her talk).

So which do you need? A mentor is useful to get you to the next level by helping you develop new skills and think through your career goals. A sponsor is a good fit if you're looking for an advocate and someone who can help you achieve more visibility in your organization.

There are no wrong answers. You'll very likely need both over the course of your career, so the decision is more about whom you need right now.

Informal, Pragmatic, and Aspirational Mentors

Personally, I have many people who I consider mentors, whom I never formally asked to mentor me—people I built relationships with, people who saw potential in me. They are people who, when they give me advice, I'm going to take what they say to heart. I follow through on the feedback they give me, and I give them updates on my life.

I like to call these "**Mentor Moments**." I have many people in my network with whom I've built relationships and know I can reach out to for help or a quick question any time.

My experience is not unusual. "I always say you don't need 10 sponsors. It's not like a Taylor Swift concert where we're exchanging friendship bracelets," says Mita Mallick, bestselling author of *Reimagine Inclusion*. For her, these relationships often come up naturally. "It just happens with the work and building the relationship."

Communications expert Vinh Giang recommends having what he calls pragmatic and aspirational mentors.

"An aspirational mentor is someone like Elon Musk or Oprah Winfrey. They're 1,000 steps ahead of you. A pragmatic mentor is 10 steps ahead of you," says Vinh. For example, when Vinh's social media following was at the 50,000 mark, he looked at those with 150,000 followers as pragmatic mentors. For Vinh, he didn't even need to reach out to learn something. "Sometimes, looking at people 10 steps ahead from afar, you can see their methodology," he shared with me.

Where to Find Them

It's not always obvious whom you should ask to become your mentor or sponsor. Most people look to folks they work with directly, but if you expand your vision a little bit, many more candidates may appear.

"Where do you go to church or temple? Where do you volunteer? What about family members? Or alumni?" points out Mita Mallick. "There's so many ways that, if you did an audit, you could find a mentor."

Particularly for mentorship, looking at someone who is outside your current place of work can give you a more objective perspective. Take a look at your existing network to see if someone might be a good fit.

People you already have a good relationship with can be a strong candidate. Carlo Dela Fuente, who is the chief of staff and director of Business Operations for Webex Product Management and Artificial Intelligence at Cisco, chose someone he had already been working with for years.

"I think sponsors have to feel comfortable putting their own brand and reputation on the line on your behalf. That doesn't happen with just, 'Hey, can you be my sponsor?' You have to really know the person's work," says Carlo. "A lot of that is done through relationship building. It takes time and effort. So you have to find ways to build relationships, to get proximate to the people you want to be sponsored by. Slowly build a foundation wherever you can, whether it be work related or personal. And then start to plant seeds around sharing the goals that you have and whether or not they can help. It's not an overnight thing."

Before you begin looking, you should be clear about what your goals are. Having specific goals will not only help you narrow down who might be a good fit but will also help the person you approach understand how they can help you.

Finally, for a mentor or sponsor, make sure you make it easy for them. You're probably approaching this person because they're successful and busy, so whatever you can do to minimize their time commitment (scheduling meetings, providing updates, etc.) will make it easier for them to accept your request.

When Paul Park, now chief revenue officer at Sparrow, approached his CEO at a previous company to mentor him, he made sure to pay attention to the details. "He asked if we could have a scheduled 30-minute call every couple of weeks. I would always put together an agenda and say what specific aspects of the business I'm trying to understand," Paul shared with me.

Paul also made sure to help the CEO where he could. "He viewed mentorship as a two-way street. He'd say, 'There's stuff I can learn from you and what your folks are doing in sales.'"

When a more junior employee mentors a more experienced colleague, it's called "reverse mentoring" and is becoming increasingly popular. Remember that just because someone is more senior doesn't mean you don't have something valuable to offer in return!

Rejection Can Be...Therapy?

Whether you're looking for a sponsor, networking, or finding people to support your bid for promotion, it's inevitable that someone will turn you down. Most people are terrified of this happening, but it's also true that every successful person experiences rejection at some point.

Author Jia Jiang (who has an excellent TED Talk called "What I Learned from 100 Days of Rejection") points out that it's how you handle rejection that matters and, in particular, the fear of rejection: "Because we have the yearning for belonging, a lot of times we don't want to rock the boat. We don't want to feel like we asked a question that's too rude or intrusive. That's why we reject ourselves more than anyone else," Jia shared with me.

Jia has embraced the concept of "rejection therapy," where you actively seek out rejection so that it no longer feels bad. He's done things like request a discount on a purchase or ask a random stranger to give him $100.

"It's okay to get rejected because you give people freedom to reject you. By giving people the freedom to reject you, you earn the freedom to ask a lot more," says Jia.

How to Expand Your Network

Like public speaking, the idea of "networking" is something that fills many people with dread. People who don't like networking (or haven't done much of it) feel like the process is contrived or transactional. A lot of the time they're simply nervous about it or don't know how to do it in a way that feels authentic.

It's helpful to look at networking from two perspectives: building relationships with people inside your current organization and meeting people outside of it.

Networking Internally

Relationships are key if you want to get your work supported and your ideas pushed forward. Networking internally is a long-term game, so it's best to focus on quality rather than quantity. Most people make the mistake of going in without a particular goal, which adds to feelings of uncertainty. Remember why you want to develop these relationships to help you push past anxiety or ambiguity.

"I am never excited to see a coffee chat on my calendar," says content creator and advisor Natalie Marshall (better known as Corporate Natalie). "But the ones that make me feel like it's a good use of my time are when I come prepared. The key is that, when they're giving you their time, you have something to give in return."

Networking should extend beyond just the people you work with. Look for opportunities to make connections with people across the organization who share an interest with you that's not directly related to your role.

"I've found that finding safe spaces to practice that also have high visibility helps," says Carlo. "My involvement in our inclusive communities have been great places and safe places to make connections across the company. Especially now in the virtual and hybrid work world, building those relationships and meeting people across the company becomes really hard."

Here are three simple things you can do to build your internal network:

- **Meet with coworkers one-on-one to build trust:** Trust is a foundational piece of any workplace relationship. The first time I had to announce a new initiative with the wider team, I was overwhelmed about getting people's commitment in a large group setting. Thankfully, I had built many strong relationships and could turn to each person beforehand. I listened to their concerns and got their buy-in at one-on-one meetings so that the official meeting would run smoothly.

- **Find an extroverted buddy:** This will be someone who likely knows a lot about most people because of their social and outgoing personality. Ask them to help make connections by sharing what you have in common with your coworkers.

- **Be patient:** Building rapport takes time. Each time I've started a new job, I've felt uptight and stressed about how everyone seemed to be friends already. Give it time and you will also find your people at work.

The Power of the Informational Interview

A tactic I love, whether networking internally or externally, is the informational interview. It sounds like what it is—an interview to learn more about that person, a company, or a specific topic (versus a regular interview, which happens after you've applied for a job). These interviews help you expand your network, learn new insights, and even help you in your job search.

During my junior year of college, I was an intern at the ad agency Leo Burnett. During the six months I was there, I set up dozens of informational interviews to learn about the business and different types of jobs, ending each interview with the question, "Who else should I meet?" My managers came away very impressed with my commitment to learning.

"I'm looking to buy lunch" is how Ross approaches people. He makes sure to do some research on who he approaches and briefly explains who he is. "Send it to five different people because you're probably not going to get them all. These people will help you in more ways than you realize down the line. I ended up getting a job through one person I met this way."

151

Building Influence at Any Level

Networking Externally

Meeting and interacting with new professional connections is one of the best ways to grow your career. For introverts, though, networking isn't typically how we want to use our free time.

"A lot of introverts, including myself, get hung up on how much people are going to care. We tend to be a little bit more empathetic. We're sitting there reading all the different ways this could go wrong—and we end up crippled by empathy," says Ross. "We tend to be afraid that we're bothering other people, even if we wouldn't feel that way if the roles were reversed."

Here are some networking tips that are effective *and* will preserve your energy:

- **Check out the attendee list:** Do you see someone you'd like to speak to? Send them a note on LinkedIn or email them ahead of the event and let them know you'd like to meet them. Or if you're unable to make the event, email them after the fact and ask if they'd be open to meet over coffee or a video chat. Whenever I do this, people come up to *me* first because they recognize me from my LinkedIn note!

- **Bring a buddy:** Mita Mallick has a great strategy. "Start the night together and then disperse. At some point, if the event isn't of value, you have an escape plan or you have someone to be accountable to," she says.

- **Embrace conversational threading:** A lot of networking conversations fall flat because the questions that are asked are those that elicit "yes" or "no." As mentioned in the previous chapter, conversational threading helps keep conversations going by giving the question asker multiple "threads" to pull from. Think about how you can answer a person's question so that they have a natural follow-up to keep the conversation flowing.

Two Networking Challenges

Vinh's students struggle with approaching new people, so he invented this three-part challenge for them:

1. Greet somebody new and say "hello." That's it. Say, "Hi, how's your day going?"
2. Level two is to say "Hi, how's your day going?" plus a compliment.
3. Level three is to say "Hi, how's your day going?" plus a compliment and a question.

"My students who do follow through and go out and just talk to one new person a day, if they do that for three or four months, it completely changes who they are," says Vinh.

Paul Park is someone who built his career off his superb networking skills, but that doesn't mean it came naturally to him. "I don't think most people ever wake up one day and say they're comfortable networking," he told me. Even though he gets energy from it, Paul still has to psych himself up—go to the bathroom, splash water on his face, and get into the right mental space.

One day, a colleague suggested an activity that excited him. "He said to me, 'Paul, let's do this. Let's start at one end of the room and let's walk all the way to the bar at the other end. Along the way, let's talk to as many people as we can.' It felt like we were gamifying things! It felt like we couldn't get that drink until we talked to every single person between us and the bar."

Grab my Outreach Organizer to jot down who you want to meet inside your company and who you want to meet outside your

Building Influence at Any Level

organization at unforgettablepresencekit.com. (You can use this organizer for the LinkedIn chapter, too!).

Discussion Questions

1. What is one aspect of the RAVE Model that I will try to get better at in the next 3 months?

2. Would I benefit more from a mentor or a sponsor?

3. Who can I ask to be a mentor or sponsor? Where should I look?

4. Which coworkers would I like to develop a stronger personal relationship with?

5. Which new networking tactic will I use the next time I go to an event?

Chapter 9

Managing Your Manager

When the pandemic began, Brenda had been working with her manager Katie for nearly a year and had built a strong working relationship—or so she had thought.

Throughout her time at the company, Brenda was driven and consistently produced great results. However, when the pandemic hit, something shifted in their relationship. Katie began micromanaging her, constantly checking in about her progress. This understandably frustrated Brenda, so much so that she wondered if it made sense for her to stay at the company.

While there are many people you will need to impress as you advance in your career, the most important is likely your direct manager. When you have a good relationship with your manager, they can be a potent combination of mentor, sponsor, confidante, and cheerleader. When you don't, it can feel like you're dragging a heavy weight behind you and can quickly lead to burnout.

The shifting dynamic between Brenda and Katie is not uncommon, especially in virtual work environments. While it was natural for Brenda to be frustrated and want to minimize the number of interactions she had with Katie, the solution to fixing her problem was to do the opposite. Brenda needed to lean *into* the relationship with her manager rather than try to avoid it. She had to learn to manage her manager.

Let me explain. Managing up is one of the most important skills that differentiates a "doer" from a strategic collaborator, leader, and partner. It's something that creates better working relationships, and can help you grow your career even faster.

Unfortunately, it's not a skill that's taught in school. For many of us, we enter the working world thinking our manager is there to assign work, help us solve issues, and determine whether we get promoted. While this is true, this is a passive relationship.

To take ownership of your career, you need to manage up—which means you need to make your manager's life as easy as possible for them.

"Managing up means you're not expecting your manager to have everything nicely defined, packaged up, and placed on a silver platter on your desk," says Wes Kao, cofounder of Maven.

It's easy to forget that your manager has a lot of other things going on—probably several other team members (with their own demands for attention), the needs of their own manager, and navigating their own career. We shouldn't expect (or want) our managers to be the single point of failure for our careers.

That's why understanding your manager and what *they* need—and working to help them achieve it—will really make you stand out. You'll instantly go from being one of their many problems to being a solution.

"The better I do, the better they do, the better we do," explains Soni Basi, a former global chief people officer at Edelman. "We get more budget, we get more opportunity, we get more visibility."

In Brenda's case, this meant having an honest conversation with Katie about what Katie wanted from her. It turned out that Katie was really struggling with the loss of visibility into Brenda's work that happened when the team had moved to remote work. She was someone who wanted more frequent communication and updates. Once Brenda learned that and became more proactive with an end-of-day summary, Katie took a step back. Because Brenda took the initiative to find out what Katie's needs were and changed her behavior accordingly, their working relationship improved.

It can be a beautiful partnership. Understanding your manager and developing a strong relationship with them will not only remove obstacles for you but also reflect well on both of you—your success is also their success, so there's no one who has a more vested interest in your advancement than your manager. In this chapter you'll learn how to build a strong foundation for this crucial relationship, one that you can both use as a launch pad.

Building Your Relationship

Of all your workplace relationships, the one with your manager deserves the most attention. Investing time in getting to know each other, and what you both want, is going to help you be seen and excel.

"Remember that your manager is a human being with their own sets of feelings," says Kim Scott, author of *Radical Candor*. "When I think of the people I know who've been most successful in their career, they respond to their manager at a human level."

When you first start working with a new manager, take some time to learn about their life and their interests (and offer up a few details about yours). Everyone wants to be seen as more than their job, so showing an interest in who they really are will at least earn you some goodwill (and will make your time together more fun too). Over time, their trust in you will increase.

Know Your Manager's Goals and Work Style

Everyone is eager to share their goals with their manager (and we'll talk more about this later in the chapter), but people often forget that their manager has goals too. Ask about their challenges, their vision, and what they're being measured on. Knowing this will help you help them, which already puts you ahead of most people. This isn't just a "nice to know" item—once you know their goals, you can align your work so that it helps them achieve those goals. This is really making sure you're being thoughtful about your team's priorities, so it will achieve several purposes: helping your team succeed, making you look good, and demonstrating your value to your manager and the company.

Not sure where to begin? Here are a few questions you can ask:

- How can I best support you?
- What do you view as success in your role?
- What are your top three to five priorities and which is the most important?
- What is the number one challenge that's getting in the way of you reaching your goals?

It's also important to know how they like to work. This can encompass several dimensions: their personality, what drives them professionally, and communication preferences. Are they introverted or extroverted? Do they really like to dig into the weeds, or do they prefer to look at projects at a high level? Do they want you to share frequent updates or only share if there's a problem you need help with?

Once you understand their goals and preferences, it will be easier for you to find ways to support them.

Knowing Me, Knowing You

A great way to help your manager or colleagues understand you better is to create a README—a personal operating manual that describes your working style, how you like to give and receive feedback, your hobbies, and anything else you'd like to share.

It can be as flexible and detailed as you want it to be. Do you like to receive emoji reactions after sending a message to know someone read it? Do you prefer quick phone calls over video meetings? Perhaps you want to share more about your style of giving feedback. This manual is going to remove a lot of potential friction caused by misunderstandings or different ways of working, and it can even help bring you all closer together as a great team bonding exercise (I led a session with the wider marketing team, and I learned so much about everyone, including a coworker who didn't like small talk, another who worked out during his lunch hour, and one who preferred group meetings during her afternoons). If your manager doesn't already have one, share yours and suggest that you'd love to understand her better by seeing what she would include in her README.

It's also meant to be a living document, so keep updating the manual as things come up or your way of working changes.

Set and Manage Expectations

Many people make the mistake of thinking that their job is to say "yes" to whatever their manager asks them to do. It's not! Doing this will hurt you in the long run by creating unreasonable expectations and causing you to burn out from too much work.

Instead, be clear about your capacity. When you agree to take on work, set realistic goals and deadlines. While it can feel good in the short-term to promise to overdeliver, it's better to promise something that you know you can accomplish and then try to beat your estimate. If it looks like something will get in the way of what you promised—like unexpected work that's come in or a personal situation that pops up—give your manager **as much advance notice as possible** so they can plan accordingly.

In general, it's better to be transparent, even when things don't go according to plan. You might be thinking: "Won't I look bad if I show that I made a mistake? Isn't it better if I fix it first?" While this is a nice solution in theory, what happens more often than not is that complex problems can't get fixed right away, which means you've delayed your manager from being able to step in and help—or worse, they find out about the problem from someone else first.

Providing an initial timeline that doesn't feel ambitious can be uncomfortable, but your manager will appreciate an accurate picture of the future. When they present you with a task, you can manage expectations by saying something like: "I'm happy to take this on, although my plate is full with project X. Can you let me know which projects take priority and if there are any non-negotiable deadlines?"

And, if you really want to stand out, be proactive with your own recommendations about the best approach to complete the work. You likely know best about what needs to be done and how long it will take.

Communicate Often

Understanding the best ways to communicate with your manager is key to a successful relationship. Knowing how frequently to check in, what kind of updates they want, and the best channels to reach them will all help to make things run smoothly.

A good rule of thumb is when in doubt, send an update—too little information is usually a much bigger problem than too much. Here's an example of an update for a non-critical project:

FYI (no action needed): There is a chance the project needs to be pushed back another week due to a vendor issue. However, I'm working with their team to see if we can avoid this. I will continue to keep you updated on our progress.

The best vehicle for communication is usually your one-on-one meetings. These should be every week or two (depending on your preference and your manager's schedule) and are a good space to get into how you're feeling about the work. We'll do a deep dive into how to set up your one-on-ones in the next chapter.

Skip-Level Meetings

While it's important to build a strong relationship with your manager, don't overlook your manager's manager. Many tech companies embrace the concept of a "skip-level meeting," where you book some time to speak with your manager's manager. The goal is to build the relationship, understand their priorities (and, by extension, your manager's), and show off your initiative.

Many people get nervous about asking for time from a busy executive. But most don't realize that you are helping the executive, too. You can offer a more holistic view of your team and a firsthand "view from the front line" that often isn't available to them otherwise.

Start small: Ask for a 15-minute meeting and come prepared with specific questions. Let your manager know it's happening, and they may be able to help you prepare.

Building these relationships and understanding an executive's perspective are important for your career development. In some cases, these conversations can be the gateway to finding important sponsors or mentors.

Here are some questions you can ask:

- What are your goals and priorities right now?
- What challenges are you facing, and how can I help?

(continued)

(continued)

- How do you see the company's goals evolving over the next three to five years?

Don't forget that they may use this as a time to ask you questions, too. Prepare for questions like these:

- What are you working on right now?
- What are your career goals and how can we support you?
- What challenges or roadblocks are your team currently facing?
- What can the leadership team do to improve communication and collaboration?

Going for Promotion

When Carlo Dela Fuente applied for his first management position at Cisco, he felt confident. As a top performer with consistently high ratings, he thought he had proven his ability to do the job. Then, Carlo got passed over for the role—twice—a runner-up each time.

Carlo would later find out that there was a piece of constructive feedback that was getting in the way of his promotion. But instead of taking more time to figure out how to address the constructive feedback to create a perfect application, he decided to lean into his strengths—and find the right stakeholders to help him make his case.

"Instead of saying, 'That's who I am and I need to address it,' I thought, 'Okay, I'll take that feedback moving forward, but at the same time, I'm getting all of these validations from other stakeholders and other people in my network. Those are just as powerful, if not more powerful, right? I'm not going to please everyone.'"

When Carlo applied for the position the third time, he changed his approach by turning to his employee resource group sponsors—many of whom reported to the CEO—who knew the work he was doing around professional development and asked them to write a letter of recommendation to the hiring manager.

"That helped me get over that first hump," says Carlo, who has since risen in the ranks to become an executive at Cisco.

Carlo didn't fall into the trap that so many of us can—trying to make everything perfect before we reach for that next step. Remember, if you were 100% ready to take on that next role, you wouldn't learn anything new once there.

This can be a particularly difficult adjustment for women in similar positions. You may have heard that men apply for a job if they meet 60% of the criteria, while women feel that they need to hit 100%. This also applies to asking for help—according to the LinkedIn Gender Insights Report, women are 26% less likely to ask for a referral than men.[1]

Your manager will be a crucial partner in preparing for your promotion (yes, it takes preparation!) and supporting you throughout the process. But they are also the person you need to convince that you're ready for the next step. The reality is that a promotion is not about the hard work that you've put in. You need to present your case clearly to your manager and ensure that you're helping your manager accomplish *their* goals.

Promotions rarely just "happen," especially as you enter senior levels. They are often a monthslong process that you can influence. The first step is understanding what you need to do.

Express Your Interest

My teammate Amanda always impressed me—she was well-liked by everyone and was a reliable teammate who did great work. She had been at the company a few years, and I had wondered why she hadn't gotten promoted yet. Then one day I came into work and she was! I immediately congratulated her, not expecting to learn one of the most important lessons of my career.

She shared that her boss had told her she hadn't gotten promoted sooner because he didn't know she wanted to be. Once she made her career aspirations clear, she got it! I was shocked. As an ambitious professional, I figured that managers would assume everyone wanted to get promoted. Turns out, it's important to be explicit about what you want. Remember: As CEO of your own career, never assume anything.

You'll want to be intentional about when you raise the topic of a promotion. Your one-on-one is the most natural time, but don't wait to initiate the conversation a month before the regular performance review cycle. You want to speak with your manager at least six months in advance to work on your goals and to figure out the key stakeholders you need support from.

Create Your Promotion Plan

Once you've made it clear you want to reach that next step in your career, you and your manager can go through the requirements and make an honest assessment of what skills you need to develop or improve and what opportunities might help you develop those skills.

Jenny Wood, founder of Google's Own Your Career program, suggests keeping a running document of all your key contributions and accomplishments. This can include links to important documents and even screenshots of impactful emails. Having a running record of your accomplishments will be a huge help when it's time for your performance review.

If your company has a career ladder, which describes the skills and behaviors required for people on the next rung, this is a great tool to guide the conversation. Go through the career ladder and assess which requirements you already have and which you still need to develop. If your company doesn't have one, try making one: ask your manager what they think the characteristics a person at the next level should have.

This becomes especially important when trying to show that you're capable of performing at the next level.

"A lot of people want a promotion, and they're still in the mindset of the job that they're in," says Linda Tong, CEO of Webflow. "But every promotion application typically says, 'Are they already demonstrating readiness for the next role?'"

This becomes your road map—a tangible set of outcomes you need to achieve. For each one, you can work with your manager or other advisors on what needs to happen. Should you get a mentor who is an expert in this skill? Should you take on a new project that will help you refine your planning skills or your experience in leading a meeting? Define your goals and set a measurable outcome that will tell you whether you've achieved the goal. This could be a quantitative measure (e.g. leading a weekly meeting of 10 people for six months) or a quality measure (e.g. collect peer feedback on the growth of your public speaking abilities).

Your manager is not the only person you should be speaking with about getting to the next level. Peer feedback is often a crucial component of your performance review, and you want to start thinking about who else will be involved in the decision. Is it your team members? Your manager's boss? The head of your discipline? There can be some strategy involved, and it'll be helpful to ask your manager whose feedback they think will have the biggest influence during your review to make sure you're set up well.

To keep improving on the key skills you need to earn you that promotion, find your "feedback circle." These are people whose opinions you value and respect and who you know will be willing to share hard truths with you.

Let your feedback circle know that you're working on improving certain skills.

For example, you could ask, "I'm working on conveying more confidence when I give presentations by being more intentional with my body language. The next time I present in a team meeting, can you please let me know if my hand gestures and pacing made me seem more confident?"

By giving your coworker that heads up, they'll be more present during the meeting and be able to give you more specific and helpful feedback. They're also likely to be more invested in your success because they've been made aware of your goals.

Preparing for Your Review

Going up for promotion is a lot less stressful if you're prepared—speaking with your manager every month, checking in with your feedback circle, and having a clear idea of what the process is like. The work you've done to improve your presence will stack the deck in your favor.

Every organization has a slightly different performance review process, but it generally involves a few core elements:

- A self-evaluation
- Your manager's input
- Peer feedback

Your self-evaluation is your chance to tell your story. Early in my career, I made the mistake of writing down every single thing I worked on in my annual review—which diluted the *actual* high-impact work I did. Instead, you need to curate your review with the most impactful things you've done. Each of those things should be tied to one of the larger goals for your organization. What's important is not what you did, but the effect it had on the company. Try to be as quantitative as possible and tie it to metrics. The goal is to leave little doubt that you've had a significant impact.

Likewise, be proactive with your manager about how you want them to support you. If they're being vague with their praise, it can actually undermine your case—you want them to reiterate the concrete impact that you've had and evaluate how you compare to your peers at your same level.

Finally, many companies give you the opportunity to provide peer or 360° feedback. This may have the biggest impact of all, as these people are generally regarded as more objective. As Carlo shared in his story, if a broad cross-section of team members are saying that you're having a big impact and are ready to make the jump to the next level, it's very hard for someone to argue with them. Remember to ask those who are more senior to you and those who are cross-functional, and let them know that you're up for promotion so that they can make the strongest case possible for you.

The Three Rs of Feedback

While giving feedback is a "gift," receiving it can sometimes feel like a present you want to return. While we all know that constructive feedback is good for us—particularly if it comes with good intentions from people we respect—receiving it often feels like eating our vegetables.

Ideally, you want to be asking for feedback all the time, not just when you want a promotion. It can be hard to ask for something that you might not enjoy hearing, but the benefits make it worthwhile. You're asking for candid feedback because it will help you improve, but it will also positively affect how people see you. The very act of

167

asking for it tells people that you are receptive to their point of view, that you value their opinion, and that you want to improve and grow. In my experience, people who ask for feedback are my favorite people to work with because they have a growth mindset and are open to learning and improving.

Your approach to receiving feedback will have a big impact on its "flavor," so I'm sharing my special recipe: the three Rs of receiving feedback: request it, reflect on it, and respond.

Request It

When asking for feedback, you want to make it as easy as possible for someone to provide it. Most people don't realize that asking for feedback *is also hard for the person you're asking it from.* You're adding something to their to-do list. They may not want to tell you something negative. Most people are uncomfortable making you feel uncomfortable, so it's easier for them to say nothing.

Fortunately, there's an easy shortcut. Rather than ask for feedback, ask for *advice.*

The word "feedback" comes with negative connotations, while the word "advice" makes us think of collaboration, support, and guidance. For the feedback asker, it's a less intimidating way to learn how you can improve. The feedback giver will feel more comfortable sharing what they really think. Who doesn't love feeling like their opinion is valued?

You can also remove any potential discomfort by changing a single word in your request.

Instead of asking "What could I have done better?" ask: "What could I have done *differently?*" This way you're removing any implication that something was not done right, which makes a feedback giver feel more comfortable with being honest.

Remember that you don't need feedback about *every* aspect of your presence or your work. Keep in mind the goals that you've set, and ask for feedback that will help you reach them.

Reflect on It

Okay, you've got some feedback, and it's not what you hoped for. It never feels good to be criticized, even if you know there's truth to it.

It can be difficult to take in feedback while your emotions are swirling, so the first step is to really listen and take in what the person is saying.

Andrew Seaman, LinkedIn editor for job searches and careers, learned an important lesson about this in his seventh-grade math teacher's room.

"There was a poster that said, 'Are you listening? Or are you just waiting to talk?' It taught me that it's important to make sure that you're really taking in what people are saying," says Andrew.

Assume that the feedback is given with the best intentions. Feedback givers have no idea how you'll respond, and there's a risk that their feedback could negatively impact your relationship. They need to find the right time to do it and communicate the feedback clearly so it doesn't feel personal. There are a lot of moving pieces, and this stress makes it easy for the words to come out wrong.

"Whenever we get constructive feedback, the fact that it's constructive will always hurt a little bit," says Wes. "We just have to recognize that bias in ourselves and not dismiss the feedback by saying, 'Well, that person could have been nicer.' In your mind, it could always be nicer. If there's a grain of truth in the feedback, try to take it without getting defensive about how they said it."

While hearing what you could do better may not feel great, remember why you asked for feedback. You have specific goals that you're trying to achieve, and these unbiased insights are going to help you achieve those goals faster. Feedback is your fuel, helping you reach your potential as quickly as you can.

Your emotions are going to be a little heightened, but that's natural. Take time to process and reflect on what you've heard before you respond.

Respond

In general, people giving feedback are doing so because they want you to succeed. They care enough about you to take the time to share so that you don't repeat the same mistakes and you can actually improve. That's why I say that after anyone gives you feedback, always start off by saying "thank you."

Then, if you can, wait at least a day before doing anything. When you reconnect, clarify anything that may be unclear or ask any necessary follow-up questions. Once you're satisfied that you understand their message and their intent, thank them once again for doing the hard thing of being honest with you.

The next step is to decide what you want to do with the feedback. Remember, there is no obligation to act on it! It's up to you to determine if it's valuable.

"I think that it's important, with any kind of feedback, but especially feedback around things like 'executive presence,' to separate the wheat from the chaff," says Kim. "You may be getting some good feedback, but you also may be getting something biased. So you want to make sure that you understand what the person is telling you."

You can ask yourself:

- Do I agree with this?
- Do I think the feedback is fair?
- Have I received this feedback before?

- How much do I respect this person's opinion?

- How much does this person know about my work?

Finally, decide how urgently you need to take action. Is this something you need to address right away (for example, a comment that the person took offense with)? Is it about a skill that you know you need to improve, but you need more time to work on it (such as showing more confidence when leading a meeting)? Or is this a true blind spot for you that you need to pay more attention to (in which case, it would be good to ask more people about it)?

If you end up deciding to take the feedback, follow up and let the feedback giver know what you changed. This tells them that you've heard them and the effort they put into expressing the feedback was well spent. It also makes them feel good that they've helped you, and they will be more likely to do it again.

The Review Process Is Not Inclusive (But You Can Help)

Many corporate rituals are a little strange when you think about them, so it shouldn't be a surprise that the review process can feel a little mysterious and opaque—it often is.

This can be especially true for people who come from different cultural backgrounds. For many people, the process of self-promotion and asking for feedback can feel like it's going against their cultural values and how they were raised.

Jerry Won, founder of World Class Speakers, explained an excellent way to reframe how to stand out in corporate America:

"It's understanding that much of the advice our parents gave us was incomplete information and a lack of understanding of how this

(continued)

(continued)

game is played. My parents' rulebook for success is influenced by how people achieved success in Korea in the '60s and '70s when they were growing up, where everybody was poor.

"The path out of that class was through respect and status-based positions. That formula overlaid into the very, very bizarre world of American corporate politics doesn't transfer."

"It's okay to respect and honor your parents and to completely disregard every little thing they tell you, because we have more information than they do. Should we not evolve and make ourselves better with more information? That sets the premise for understanding how this game is played."

Bias also plays a role in this discomfort. A 2022 study from MIT called "Potential and the Gender Promotion Gap" points out that "on average, women received higher *performance* ratings than male employees but received 8.3% lower ratings for *potential* than men. The result was that female employees on average were 14% less likely to be promoted than their male colleagues."[2]

This is frustrating and can leave women in particular feeling powerless. If you're in a leadership position, one tactic to help level the playing field is to look out for deserving candidates, who might not otherwise put themselves forward, and "nominate" them for advancement. It's also important if you're a woman to know that this bias exists, as understanding it can empower you to take intentional steps to ensure your work and ambitions are seen and valued.

Discussion Questions

1. Do I know my manager's priorities?

2. How can I improve how I communicate with my manager?

3. Have I had a productive conversation with my manager about my career goals?

4. What do I need to include in my promotion plan?

5. What kind of feedback would help me to improve and who should I ask for it?

Part IV

Leadership and Management

Chapter 10

Thinking Like a Manager

In the hilarious sitcom *Superstore*, Amy Sosa (played by America Ferrera) works her way up from floor clerk in a big-box store all the way to store manager over several seasons. On her first day in the new role, she's excited to start off on the right foot (and very excited by the generous new salary). However, things don't go quite like she imagined.

Her old manager interrupts her at the morning staff meeting and has to be reminded that he's not the manager anymore. She hires a new assistant, who accidentally hands her new contract to the PA announcer, who then reads out her new salary to the entire store. Her staff, already mad that one of their former colleagues now makes a lot more money than they do, gets even angrier when they find out that she also gets an expensive corporate car. Frustrated with Amy's new stature, one of her staff guilts her into paying for a customer's order.

Becoming a manager is a big moment in anyone's career. It often represents years of hard work and growth. While there's a lot to look forward to, it also comes with some growing pains.

I was wracked with nerves on my first day as manager. It's a change in how others see you and how you see yourself, but most importantly, it means you have to start thinking differently. Your presence is no longer just defined by your own actions—you represent a team, and that team represents you. Their wins are your wins. This can be both intimidating and an opportunity—if you can learn how to run your team smoothly, you'll make an even larger impression than you ever have.

One of the earliest battles many new managers have is with imposter syndrome. "The higher we go in our careers, the more imposter syndrome we have," says author and former Google executive Jenny Wood. "You're surrounded by people of high caliber."

This is natural, but you can push past it by being prepared, having a clear plan for how to manage, and embracing the fact that some things just need to be learned on the job. In this chapter we'll look at key strategies you can use to get the most out of the people you manage and to rally your team behind you. Before long, all the impressive work you did to get to this stage will be magnified, and your profile will grow.

First, however, you have to learn to think differently.

Adopting a Manager's Mindset

When I first became a manager, I felt uptight and constantly nervous that I was doing the job incorrectly. I put immense pressure on myself, thinking that I had to immediately be the problem solver and motivator, ready to hit the ground running, with all my goals laid out—all completely unrealistic expectations for someone new to the role (and on top of that, I was also new to the company). While a manager's job is to do and be all of those things eventually, it's also important to remember that you're a person who's learning, just like everyone else on your team.

The biggest mindset shift you make when you're a manager is to *avoid* doubling down on all the skills and behaviors that got you to this point. Being a manager is a different kind of job—it's not doing the same kind of work output. It's a people-oriented job. Your role is more like a conductor who makes sure everything is moving as it should be. You're supporting your team execute on the work, while also making sure the right work is getting done and done well. Your job is to make sure your team has the resources they need to thrive and succeed.

This dependency on your team leads many new managers into a common trap: becoming a micromanager. Of course, this doesn't work. It will slow your team down and they'll become frustrated, while both output and morale will decrease. Instead, you need to empower them and let people see what they can do. Your team will feel more ownership over their work and find solutions that achieve their goals as well as the goals of the business. Autonomy is a great catalyst to build confidence and resilience.

Empowering your team helps build an environment of psychological safety. When employees feel psychologically safe, they can speak up and take calculated risks without fear of retribution. This can lead to more innovative ideas and solutions. Famously, when Google's People Operations team studied what contributed the most to the success of their teams, the answer was psychological safety.

Creating psychological safety is just part of one of your biggest jobs as a manager: earning your team's trust.

Practice Swift Trust

The quickest way to earn trust from your team is to give it—swiftly.

This can feel uncomfortable. Many new managers think, "Shouldn't people earn my trust?" This is often why people get nervous when they get a new boss. They think they have to prove themselves and earn their trust from scratch.

This can be particularly hard in a virtual or hybrid environment. When we used to all go into the office, trust was based on what we saw. Were people early? Did they leave late? Were they working hard at their desks or distracting coworkers with stories from their weekend? All of these signals (and others, like body language) disappear when you rarely share a physical space.

To counteract this, try showing your colleagues that you trust them *before* they've earned it. This swift trust will allow you and your team to work faster and better together right from day one. When you trust your team, it means you delegate more, which builds even more trust and helps your teammates grow their skills. You're creating a virtuous circle.

Another way to show trust is through transparency.

"What works really well is being honest with my manager and my skip-level managers, but also my direct reports to say: 'I'm not hiding anything from you, I'm going to try and be as upfront with communication as possible,'" says Andrew Seaman, LinkedIn editor for job searches and careers. "That way, people in leadership know exactly what's going on. And people who are under me in the chain of command also trust that I'm not pulling the wool over their eyes."

Lead with Empathy and Authenticity

Part of the transition to becoming a manager is realizing that your work is about people, not the tasks you have to complete.

When leading with empathy, start by getting to know your team as individuals. Learn about their strengths, their challenges, and their goals in life, both personally and professionally. By building relationships and learning about your team, you can support them more effectively. Avoid the routine questions we always ask on calls and instead, think about starting each meeting with questions like, "How are you doing with all the changes this week?" and "What's on your mind?" and show them that you *actually* want to hear the answer.

"I try and take the time to talk to people a little bit about their personal life and I share personal things about my own life because I truly believe it makes work more fun and more satisfying when you have deeper connections with people," says Christina Hall, chief people officer at Instacart.

During the first three months in your new role, your most important job will be to listen, learn, ask questions, and then ask more questions. Whether you're at a new company or you just got promoted, pretend like you're starting from ground zero. Here are some good questions to start with for each person on your team:

- How do you like to be rewarded?
- What do you like to do outside of work?
- How do you like to receive feedback, written or face-to-face?
- How do you like to be acknowledged and praised? Publicly? Privately?
- What part of your work do you like doing most and what do you like doing least?

How to Manage Your People

As a people manager, your most important job is developing and promoting the people on your team. You play a key role in helping them develop their presence.

Let's look at a few important tools.

Put Them in Charge of Your One-on-Ones

You'll want to start off meeting with your direct reports individually, ideally once a week. Especially in a remote or hybrid setup, these will be important moments of connection, learning, and bonding.

The most important thing to communicate is that this time should be led by your direct report. They need to know that this meeting is on the calendar so you can solve problems collaboratively, talk about their career goals, and understand how you can better support them.

What to do: Ask your direct reports to create a living document that includes different sections like "Updates," "Questions," and "Challenges." This then becomes something you can easily reference again.

Why it works: Managers can read through the updates quickly and spend the majority of the one-on-one time tackling bigger issues. You can even review it before the start of the meeting to make your time together as productive as possible. It also helps your direct report stay organized, and it gives them agency by having them set the agenda for the call instead of being a passive participant.

It's also important to zoom out and look at the big picture sometimes. Once a month or so I recommend dedicating a person's one-on-one (or adding a new meeting to the calendar) to checking in on how they're progressing toward their career goals or having a larger conversation about their career aspirations. These kinds of discussions don't always come up naturally so it's important to signify their importance by regularly setting aside time for them.

Your other job is to check in on how your people are doing on a personal level. While not everyone will want to share their feelings, being comfortable sharing personal information can have a huge impact on someone's performance and job satisfaction. You never know what kind of issues outside of work may be affecting them on the job.

Here are a few questions you can ask during your one-on-ones:

- How are you feeling?
- How are you sleeping?
- Where do you need help?
- What are your career goals?

- What is your biggest challenge right now?

- How are you feeling about your workload and priorities?

- How do you feel like you're progressing against the goals you set for yourself?

Download my One-On-One Meeting Blueprint at unforgettablepresencekit.com.

Be Thoughtful About Schedules

A previous manager of mine often worked late into her evenings. Occasionally, I'd get a Slack message from her as I was winding down for the night. Even though she would tell me it wasn't anything I needed to address until the next day, I couldn't help but feel anxious thinking about what needed to be done—and I know many others have had similar experiences.

To prevent situations like these, define core working hours that overlap for your team, and then allow them to choose the rest of their working hours based on when they're most productive. This approach reduces stress and fosters a flexible work culture where people can make their presence as impactful as possible—without needing to be available at all hours. While being present contributes to presence, it doesn't mean you should always be "on."

Flexibility isn't just a nice-to-have, but something employees crave. Many studies have shown that flexibility leads to increased employee happiness and satisfaction. For example, in a Future Forum Pulse survey of 10,000 knowledge workers, 94% of people said they want flexibility about *when* they work (compared to 79% who wanted more control over *where* they work).[1]

Even when your team is working outside core hours, it's important to be mindful of how and when you communicate. For example, when I began leading a team, I made it a point to use the scheduling function for messages sent in the evening, so they wouldn't feel pressured to respond after hours.

Finally, how you communicate deadlines is just as critical to being respectful of your team's schedules. Saying you want something "by next week" or "by the end of the day" will mean different things to different teammates. To avoid confusion, always include the time, time zone, and date when requesting a deliverable. When you set specific deadlines, your teammate can tell you right away if it's something that can be met. And if not, it gives you two a chance to discuss what's actually realistic.

Remember Positive Body Language and Communication

As a manager, people are paying attention to a lot more than your words. You'll be under closer scrutiny than before since people are looking to you as a leader. This can result in your teammates finding insights or concerns in small, often inadvertent, signals you send with your body language and tone.

Your presence as a leader is going to be particularly critical. That off-handed comment you made in a meeting? It could lead a teammate to searching for something you didn't actually care about. That one-word reply? They might think you're angry. And that late-night message might signal you want your team working similar hours. While I don't want you stressing out over every little thing, I want you to be aware that your presence now has an even bigger impact on others' workload and emotions.

How to Manage Your Team

Guiding and mentoring is one important part of being a manager, but just as important is how you lead your team as a whole. Becoming a manager means you're going to have a chance to flex new muscles in setting strategy, aligning your people, and leading your team through hard challenges.

Wes Kao learned this while cofounding Maven. "As you become more senior, you'll face more ambiguous problems. You'll need to draw information out of others," says Wes. "You'll need to 'shape' projects: What is the scope? What are we going to tackle? What aren't we going to prioritize? Why does this matter? You're making a lot of decisions that shape how the rest of your team is going to execute."

Where to begin? We'll start with a few best practices that will help you make a strong initial impression with your team and get you on the road to success.

Share Goals and Expectations

As a new manager, there are two key things you need to communicate: your purpose and your goals. You need to clearly state how you plan to reach those goals and how they align with your organization's objectives.

When your team has clarity on these things, they're able to set their own goals. This understanding is a critical part of employee happiness because the anticipation of achieving a goal actually releases dopamine in our brains. Setting a well-defined goal also activates the part of our brain responsible for going after goals.[2]

Stepping into this direction-setting mindset can be a big adjustment, especially for introverts who prefer to be out of the spotlight, but it's essential.

"As a leader, it's important to project out your beliefs about how you expect things to work, and it's important for you to be able to articulate that. As a leader, that's your role," says Arin Bhowmick, chief designer officer at SAP, who describes himself as an introvert. "Unless your team members and peers know what you're thinking, it's hard to get alignment, it's hard to get credibility, it's hard to get buy-in."

Try setting up a central place to house all of this information and update it as needed. It should be somewhere easily accessible (like an internal wiki) that the team will regularly see. At the end of the day, a team without a clear North Star is a confused and unhappy team. Make sure you establish your goals and process early on to keep everyone on track.

Want to get better at setting goals? Try this exercise that bestselling business author Daniel Pink shared with me:

> *I learned this idea from [business legend] Peter Drucker. Every six months, I will write a memo where I'm projecting how I think things are going to be six months from now.*
>
> *So what will I have gotten done? How will I be feeling, etc.? Even some of the people in my midst, where are they going to be?*

*And then I don't look at it until six months later. I have
a little thing in my calendar that goes off. And I look to see,
was I right?*

This simple exercise is a great way to measure and improve your forecasting ability, which will help you set accurate goals for your team.

Boost Team Success with Pre-mortems and Post-mortems

Pre- and post-mortems allow teams to reflect on their work and identify challenges and areas for improvement. While people are more familiar with post-mortems, both approaches offer timely insights that stop your team from repeating mistakes or running into obstacles that could have been avoided.

Post-mortems are held after a project is completed. The team gathers to discuss the project from start to finish: what went well, what didn't go so well, and areas for improvement on future projects. While it's a useful exercise for helping your team learn and grow, it can also help you plan for new projects. If you're working on a project that's similar to what another team has worked on before, ask if they did a post-mortem that they can share.

Pre-mortems happen before a project even begins. This is an exercise where you gather the team, imagine that the project has failed and try to think of all the reasons why it may have happened. It's a great way to acknowledge and prepare for obstacles that stand in the way of success.

The benefit of making these exercises a regular part of your routine is that everyone has a chance to put their cards on the table. The team can make adjustments when a problem is small, rather than after it has had months to grow.

Build a Culture of Feedback

When a new manager (or even a seasoned one) asks their team open-ended questions or for general feedback, oftentimes they'll be met with a response like "It's going well" or "Everything's good." No one wants to upset their manager! But it's your job to help push your team past this discomfort if you really want them (and you) to improve. In fact, giving (and getting) feedback is one of the best ways to build your presence as a manager.

One helpful way to solicit meaningful feedback is to consistently ask for it. The first time you ask, your teammate might not feel comfortable giving you their actual opinion. Ask for it three or four more times, though, and they'll realize you're serious about wanting feedback (and they can respond the same way for only so long before it gets awkward!).

Also focus on collaborative language. Instead of asking for constructive feedback, which can make the feedback giver feel uncomfortable or wary of insulting their manager, you can ask, "I'd like your help coming up with a few ideas. What is one thing we can change or do differently next time to make sure everyone feels like they have a chance to speak up?"

Vulnerability also works really well here. For example, you might share, "I've gotten feedback before that I don't give teammates enough of a chance to ask questions during meetings. What's one thing you suggest I try out moving forward to get better at this?"

The key is to show that you really want the feedback—even if people may not believe you at first.

"You can get your team to help you by giving them permission to challenge your ideas," says Rich Mulholland, founder of Missing Link and Too Many Robots. "They won't want to challenge your ideas because they think that when they do, they're telling you that you're wrong. But they're just saying that you're no longer right."

Discussion Questions

1. How can I show my team that I trust them?

2. Am I letting my reports fully lead their one-on-ones?

3. Can I give my team more flexibility with their schedule?

4. How can I get to know my direct reports on a more personal level?

5. Have I shared my goals with my team and put this information somewhere they can easily find it?

Chapter 11

Increasing Your Team's Presence

Every Friday at Prezi, I published a newsletter to the company's internal wiki. The newsletter documented major wins, updates, and learnings—making sure to highlight each individual team member and their contributions. While soliciting that information for the newsletter added work to my team's plate (and perhaps was occasionally filled out begrudgingly), it was work they were ultimately happy to do because they understood the value. As one team member shared with me at the time, "It feels good to see the work we're doing be acknowledged and shared more widely."

When you grow as a manager and a leader, how you think about presence needs to evolve. Your goal is no longer to simply extend your own presence but to think about how and where your team shows up. At times, it will be best for you to stand up and represent your team; at other times, it will be best to stand back and let your team show what they can do.

When it's your turn to shine, not only will you be interacting with more people whom you need to influence and make a positive impression on, but each of those encounters will have a bigger impact than before because you now represent a team.

The good news is that you can continue to focus on developing the skills we've already talked about: building relationships, giving presentations, and sharing your writing with more people.

But you'll also need to learn how to boost the presence of others.

"As a people leader, my purpose is to lift people up," says Christina Hall, chief people officer at Instacart. "Sometimes you do that by letting people have the floor. Sometimes you do that by giving people more responsibility. Sometimes you do that by giving people positive feedback. Sometimes you do that by giving them clear, constructive feedback."

In this chapter, we're going to focus on four foundational management skills and how you can apply them to create a larger presence for your team. Each of these skills involves learning how to do things you haven't had to do before. The common thread is that they all involve influencing other people—leaders, your peers, and the people who report to you—to embrace your perspective and vision. As a manager, your job is to work with your colleagues to achieve the best possible outcomes. By learning to use the collective talents of the people around you, you can really make big things happen.

What's exciting is that as a team you are more powerful than you ever were as an individual. By learning how to steer your team in the right direction and grow its presence, you will unlock an even larger presence for yourself—and enjoy sharing that success with the people you work with.

Advocate for Your Team

This whole book has so far talked about advocating for yourself and becoming the CEO of your career by being intentional about your professional presence. When you become a leader, it's time to broaden that to advocate for your whole team. When you do this, you're showing the contributions of your team to leadership and the team's presence will grow.

"Part of my job is helping everyone understand the value that my team brings," says Arin Bhowmick, chief design officer at SAP. "What are they good at? What additional impact can they make? I'm giving them the backing needed for them to do their work."

In any company, there are moments that have a particularly big impact on your team's resources and success. You need to know when those moments are and be prepared to stand up for your team's interests. For example, when annual budgets are being set is a really important time to go to bat for your team and make sure that leadership understands what you need. The budget process can be a bit of a mystery, so work with your manager to learn how budgets are set and how your team's needs can get through to the decision-makers.

Another important moment is when promotions are being decided. Even if you've been promoted yourself, you may not understand how the process works—is there a committee? Who's on it? How are they making their decisions? Usually more people are up for a promotion than receive one, so how can you set your team members apart? It can take some asking around to find these answers, but knowing how the process works will make a world of difference to your reports. For example, many companies rely on testimonials from peers and other managers to make their decision, so making sure that your team knows who to ask for recommendations can make or break their case.

It's also important to teach your team how to advocate for themselves. Encouraging your people to promote their wins over chat and email is an excellent way to give them more visibility and presence in those channels (and they can use the tips in this book!). If they're nervous about how to frame things, let them know they can lean on you as their manager to provide edits and feedback before they share more widely.

Finally, there are lots of places you can celebrate your team's accomplishments to boost their presence:

- **Post your wins in smaller team channels:** It's a great morale booster and provides another avenue for individuals to be recognized. Each week, I took highlights from our team's newsletter and celebrated those teammates in Slack.

- **Volunteer to share what your team has been working on:** You can share during an all-hands meeting.

- **Tell your manager what a great job your team is doing in your one-on-ones:** Highlight specific projects or actions on a regular basis.

- **Send a congratulatory email to the team and CC other senior leaders, including your manager and even your manager's manager:** It's a more subtle (but still impactful) way to show leadership all the great work your team is doing, and both your teammates and senior leaders will appreciate it. (It works both ways: you can also share positive feedback from execs back to your team to boost their confidence.)

Remember, advocating for your team leads to recognition, opportunity, and happier teammates.

Get to Know Your Peers

When I was promoted to director, the last thing I wanted was to add more meetings to my calendar. However, I quickly realized that meetings with my peers were among the most important ones I could have.

When you become a manager, you often hear that you need to learn people management skills—how to work with the people on your team to develop their abilities and maximize their impact. This is true, but it overlooks an equally important "people skill": building relationships with other managers. This is crucial, because these relationships are the way that you advocate for your team, find opportunities for them, and learn how to become a better manager yourself. The more people you know, the larger your presence is at your company.

"It's important to have a general understanding of what your peers do," says Arin. "You'll have to step into other lanes, which are led by other managers. So it helps to have peer relationships who are open to your contributions and don't see it as a threat."

Other managers have a daily impact on your effectiveness. They can:

- Make it easier to work cross functionally with their team.
- Share best practices on things they've been successful with.
- Offer support for your voice to be heard at leadership meetings.
- Be mentors and sponsors for people on your team or your own development.
- Provide information-sharing and insights on opportunities within the organization.

When I began scheduling meetings with the other directors and senior leaders, there was rarely an agenda; the focus was on information sharing and relationship building. We would be a sounding board for the other person's challenges, discuss what was going on with our teams, or just provide a safe place to blow off steam. It was also a chance for me to share what was working for my team so that other managers could benefit from our insights. Over time, these meetings helped me to build my profile and often led to real friendships.

These relationships are often invaluable when you need to reach out for quick feedback or an honest opinion. For Soni Basi (a global chief HR officer and the former global chief people officer at Edelman), this has been an invaluable way to move her work forward.

"I don't wait for a meeting. I text them and I say, 'I've been thinking about this. What do you think? Can I grab a couple of minutes between meetings next week?' Sometimes I'll say, 'I know you're walking right now. Can I give you a quick buzz to run something by you?'" says Soni.

"It's in those moments where you really build the connection with people because, one, you've been listening to what they're doing and what their schedule is, and two, you're going after your needs in a way that doesn't feel like you're jamming it down their throat in a formalized meeting. By the time I am presenting it to the CEO for approval, I've already talked to the leadership team and they're all nodding yes."

Delegate to Make Your Team More Effective

In the long-running sitcom *Parks and Recreation*, there's an episode in season 5 where two managers decide to test whose method of delegating is more effective.

The always cheery Chris Traeger (played by Rob Lowe) focuses on encouragement, appreciation, and smiles, while the curmudgeonly Ron Swanson (Nick Offerman) is sure that offering money, fear, and deprivation will get the most out of someone.

They set up a contest to see who can make the hapless Jerry Gergich (Jim O'Heir) more effective at filing. Ron's approach gets more folders filed but also creates more mistakes. There's no clear winner.

Meanwhile, April Ludgate (Aubrey Plaza), who is supposed to undergo management training with the winner, reveals that her aim all along was "to pit Ron and Chris against each other" and sit back and watch for fun. Ron and Chris agree that she will make an excellent manager.

As a manager, you have a major impact on your team's performance. One of your most effective tools for getting more done—and boosting the visibility of your team—is knowing the right ways to delegate.

Done correctly, delegation increases the productivity of everyone on your team. For your reports, it's the chance to develop their skills and confidence (not to mention their profile). For you, it frees up your time to do higher-level work and focus on more strategic projects that will deliver the most impact. I recommend starting small by finding out what each person on your team can handle and where their strengths lie.

"Building confidence is a continuous process that involves setting small, achievable goals and celebrating each success. I call these micro-wins," says Vanessa Van Edwards, founder of Science of People. "Winning, even in a small way, can trigger a beautiful internal chemical process. So the more you feel like a winner, the more your mind and body perform like a winner. These small wins create a positive feedback loop that enhances self-assurance over time."

Deciding What to Delegate

Becoming good at delegation is a bit like becoming a matchmaker. You want to pair the right opportunity with the right person. If the task doesn't match the skill set of the person you give it to—or if they just don't have the bandwidth to do an effective job—your results will be disappointing. But if you get it right, people's confidence will soar as they take on more responsibility.

The first question to ask yourself is "What work should I delegate?" To find the answer, I think about the following:

- Is this a high-priority or a business-critical project? (If yes, keep it in your wheelhouse.)
- Will delegating this work help clear time on my calendar?
- Is this recurring work?
- Does this work require skills I lack?
- Is this work time-consuming? (Consider doing an audit of how much time each task takes you each week.)

The goal is to free up your time to do higher-level work and focus on more strategic projects (giving you a chance to have a bigger impact). A strong manager is someone who realizes that it doesn't matter who does the work; it matters that the work gets done.

You may feel like you're the only one who knows how to do the work properly. Or you may still associate your value with doing the hands-on execution work. I understand it can be tough to let these things go, but you're a manager now for a reason. You're ready to move on to more complex and interesting projects. Brendan Ittelson, chief ecosystem officer at Zoom, has an interesting perspective that I've also seen other top leaders express.

"As long as I've been at Zoom, the message that I've always told my team is I am actively trying to work myself out of a job. My number-one goal is to always be replaced because, if I'm not, I can't move to a new challenge and someone else can't move up and advance," Ittelson shared with me. "You always want to be replaceable so that you can go where the best opportunity is. That trickles down throughout my team. They're always looking at, 'How can I perform at the next level and perform strong at my level?'"

Busy schedules and a lack of time can also cause delegation challenges. My client Michael had recently been promoted to manager and was having trouble letting go of his existing tasks. He believed that it would take longer to train someone else and review the work than to handle it himself, a common concern for new managers. While this may have been true in the short term, holding onto the work was already causing long-term problems. Michael had begun experiencing burnout and because he wasn't delegating enough work, he didn't have enough time to prepare for his meetings, which hurt his credibility with the leadership team.

Instead, I recommended that he reframe the situation. It may take longer the first time you teach someone, but they'll be able to do it themselves the next time. The time you invest now will ultimately save you a lot more time in the future—and it will help your team grow and learn new skills, too.

As he began delegating more work, Michael's schedule opened up so that he had more time to prepare for high-stakes situations where he needed to show his leadership capabilities.

Who Is the Right Person for the Job?

Once you've decided what tasks to hand off, the question becomes who is best suited to the work? When "vetting" someone for an opportunity, ask these questions before handing things off:

- Is there time to redo the work if needed?
- What else is on this person's plate, and will they have the bandwidth and time to take on this new project?
- Do I have time to train them, review their work, answer their questions, and make sure they feel supported throughout the process?

- Does this work give this person an opportunity to grow and develop their skills?
- Is this work or skill area something they have expressed interest in before?

If these questions don't raise any red flags, it's usually a good idea to delegate the work to that person. Unlocking opportunities is one of your most powerful tools for boosting the confidence of your team members. By giving others the chance to shine, you'll give *them* the chance to make a powerful impression on others. If you make a practice of pushing your team into the spotlight, soon everyone will notice how you've developed a team full of stars.

Delegating can be about showing what people can do as much as getting things off your plate. For example, one of my direct reports once told me that she wanted to do more writing. Together, we created a user case study series that aligned with our company goals. The work shared valuable insights on the habits of our power users, our team's profile increased, and she got to write more. Win-win-win.

Providing your team opportunities to level up has all kinds of advantages beyond increasing their presence. It builds loyalty and enhances your whole team's capabilities, making it easier for you to accomplish more. It's also a way for you to develop and coach your team members. Studies have shown that investing in employees' career growth leads to better job satisfaction, more engaged employees, and ultimately better business outcomes. I recommend sitting down with each person on your team and finding out what their goals are and what skills they want to learn. This will help you assess the ideal work to delegate to them so that they can reach those goals.

What to Do If Things Go Wrong

No matter how good your planning is, when a team member takes on a project or assignment for the first time, there is going to be a learning curve that may result in missteps or mistakes.

It's important to remember that mistakes are part of the process. You'll just want to make sure that they don't happen too often. If you can develop a reputation for addressing mistakes quickly, that will actually *help* your team's presence.

If a mistake happens, it's important to first understand the cause. Was it your instructions? Did you give clear expectations? Was it a careless error? Or did they fail to ask follow-up questions when they didn't understand the goal of the project?

Once you have a clear understanding of *why* things didn't work out, you can offer feedback that will ensure it doesn't happen next time. We'll talk more about the right way to deliver feedback in the next section.

Even if things are not always a success, I recommend you continue to develop your team by delegating work to them. Speaking from experience, delegating work to help teammates learn new skills and take on new challenges (and then seeing them grow and thrive) is one of the most rewarding parts about being a manager. It's also an essential skill for you to develop, too.

Make Feedback Your Superpower

Of all the skills in this chapter, this one may be the most powerful. In Chapter 9 we talked about the importance of *asking* for feedback to help *your* presence. *Giving* thoughtful, regular feedback is an important part of building the presence of your team.

Many people shy away, though, because giving feedback is often difficult and uncomfortable! No one likes being the bearer of bad news. It can be especially hard for many new managers. Maven cofounder Wes Kao shared a survey from *Harvard Business Review* and Interact that found that 69% of managers often feel uncomfortable communicating with their employees, and 37% say they don't like giving direct feedback if they think the person may respond negatively.[1]

Wes has seen well-intentioned feedback go wrong many times. "The most common mistake when giving feedback is making it about yourself. Instead, you want to optimize for behavior change. This means less venting, trying to have the last word, and talking about how frustrated you are. And more sharing reasons why the person would benefit from changing their behavior."

Wes adds, "I call this 'strategy not self-expression.' Self-expression is 90% of what you initially want to say, strategy is usually 10%. That 10% is actually going to make them want to change, and have the skills and motivation to be able to do so."

This means that even if you're angry or hurt because of what the other person has done, you need to exercise self-restraint. Being strategic and presenting feedback in a structured way takes the emotion out of things and makes your feedback more actionable.

Start by explaining the reason you're giving the person feedback—to help them improve and thrive.

Adam Grant (author of many bestsellers and professor at the Wharton School) points out that research shows you can boost people's receptiveness to feedback with just 19 words: "I'm giving you these comments because I have very high expectations and I know that you can reach them."[2] This simple act shows that you believe in them and want them to succeed, which gives even hard feedback a purpose.

Let's not forget that feedback can also be positive! Publicly praising team members is part of building a strong team culture. In the office, it was easy to say "good job" or give shout-outs in passing. In a remote world, people are often missing that (and crave it!).

"I really try and be thoughtful, to take some time to acknowledge and recognize great work," says Instacart's chief people officer Christina Hall, who sends three notes of appreciation or kudos every Friday (by email, Slack, text, or even a physical note). "I get at least three nice responses back, and it starts my weekend in a really good space."

You will also benefit from sharing positive feedback more broadly. Think about a time when your teammate publicly acknowledged your hard work in that team meeting. It felt great, right? If you give someone positive feedback, take another 30 seconds and also share it in a team channel or even with your leadership group. It's a win for the feedback recipient, your team, and you (who just expanded your presence)!

Why You Shouldn't Use the Feedback Sandwich

Giving feedback can be nerve-wracking. Many of us try to minimize those nerves by using the feedback sandwich: compliment on top, feedback in between, and then another compliment on the bottom to soften the blow.

Don't do this! While the feedback sandwich may have good intentions, it hurts both of you in the long run. When people hear a compliment followed by a "but" or "however," the positive feedback suddenly feels disingenuous, or they may miss the important feedback altogether.

A more direct and transparent approach rooted in trust and focused on growth will lead to better outcomes and stronger team dynamics. Use the framework I share in the next section, or another one you like, to get comfortable giving growth-oriented feedback directly.

The FOCUS Framework

Now that you've got someone's attention, how do you present feedback well? I use what I call the FOCUS Framework, which includes a crucial element most feedback models miss:

1. **Frame it:** Provide context—what was the situation?

2. **Observe it:** Share the specific actions or behaviors that you've seen, using neutral language that focuses on the facts.

3. **Consequences:** Explain the impact of the behavior on the team or organization.

4. **Understand it:** Highlight how the feedback affects the person receiving it.

5. **Steps to take:** Outline what the person can do to change the behavior or actions you've noted.

Many feedback conversations focus more on the impact to the team or project than on the individual receiving it. However, most people are self-motivated and more likely to take action when they understand how the issue affects them personally.

Let's take the example of someone who has a problem meeting deadlines and see how the FOCUS Framework applies:

Frame it: "I've messaged you a few times on Slack about this deliverable."

Observe it: "Every time I've messaged you on the agreed upon due date, the day passes without an update from you."

Consequences: "When we miss deadlines, it slows the overall project and takes time away from my other work because I need to spend time following up with you."

Understand it: "This is causing me to lose trust in you, which makes it harder for me to give you important work."

Steps to take: "From now on, can you proactively update me if deadlines need to change and explain why? If you're facing challenges meeting a deadline or prioritizing work, let's talk to see how I can help."

"Feedback really should be about how to improve the action," says Robert Glazer, bestselling author of *Elevate, Elevate Your Team,* and *Friday Forward.* "I think you should give feedback immediately, or within 72 hours. It should be supportive, but direct."

Discussion Questions

1. Who among my management peers do I need to build a stronger relationship with?

2. What can I do to set up my team for success at critical moments?

3. What tasks am I currently doing that can be done by someone else on my team?

4. Who on my team is ready to grow by taking on new work?

5. What can I do better when giving feedback?

Chapter 12

Expert Advice on Executive Presence

Soni Basi, global chief HR officer (CHRO) and the former global chief people officer at Edelman, told me a story about her first experience with presence at the C-suite level.

When I was very early on in my career, I was a consultant for a boutique firm and had opportunities to work with C-level executives straightaway at some of the best regarded companies in the world. My very first official client meeting was with the C-suite of Merck globally (a very large pharmaceutical company). I was walking into a room where the CEO of Merck was there, and I was a little bit shell-shocked.

At that time, I'd heard that you should work on how you appear, that it has even more impact than what you say and how you say it. So I focused on absolutely nailing my appearance and nailing my presentation.

I know now that I was a little too stiff—I was so focused on looking the part and sounding the part that I was missing all the visual cues that were happening in the room. I wasn't able to hear the conversation, and I think so much about presence is how you hear the conversation that's happening in the room and how you respond to it. It's your tone of voice; it's the way in which you acknowledge others in the room and bring them in. It's the softer elements of presence that I totally didn't get back then, but you have to

*go through those experiences to really understand what it
means to be present. Part of presence is how to be present.*

Presence is a large part of being an effective executive, but the
phrase "executive presence" has always had its issues. For a long
time, it meant fitting a certain stereotype—a Caucasian middle-aged
man, in an expensive suit, who "owns the room." He has a loud
voice, a strong handshake, and instills fear when he addresses you.
He may be part of a so-called boys' club in the office with others
who look exactly like him.

"I think that anytime someone talks about executive presence,
alarm bells start going off because the term is a superhighway for
bias," says *Radical Candor* and *Radical Respect* author, Kim Scott.
"Often in my career, when people said you need to work on your
executive presence, what they really meant was, 'I wish you were a
man.'"

What defines executive presence is changing for the better, but
that doesn't mean the definition is clear cut yet. (**Pro tip:** If your
boss asks you to show more "executive presence," ask more prob-
ing questions to find out *exactly* what executive presence means to
them.) Some traits are likely always to be associated with executive presence—gravitas and polish are still important, as are being
a strong public speaker and confidence. But now more than ever,
I believe modern-day executive presence boils down to what I like to
call the three Cs of the C-suite—career brand, communication skills,
and credibility.

While we've talked about these topics throughout the book,
I also wanted you to hear firsthand experiences from executives—
these are individuals who have applied many of the skills in this
book to get to where they are today. This chapter will mainly be a
platform for these expert voices as they share their lessons from the
front lines of today's business world. Their advice shows what skills

to develop if you want to rise in the ranks and create an unforgettable presence.

Ultimately, whether you have executive presence depends on whether *others* see those traits in you. That means continuing to work on the "how" part of presence but also the "where." People's perception of you is going to be strongly influenced by how often and where they see you, which means there are many opportunities to shape that perception. The good news? Anyone can learn executive presence; it's not something we're inherently born with or that applies to a certain group, seniority, industry, or personality type.

Redefining Executive Presence

The traditional definition of executive presence is sometimes referred to in a tongue-in-cheek way as "you know it when you see it." Unfortunately, a lot of people don't see themselves in the more traditional definition of an executive I described at the start of the chapter. Part of thinking and acting like an executive is throwing out that definition and reframing it to focus more on qualities like authenticity, active listening, and empathy—which, by the way, have all been described as top descriptors of executive presence in a 2022 survey published in the Harvard Business Review.[1]

Executive presence has had a really negative connotation in my career, being a 5'1½" dark-skinned woman of South Asian descent.

I just didn't fit into what corporate America defined as executive presence. So I can remember, from when I started my career, I was assigned a coach who told me, "Always wear heels, always make sure you have shoulder pads or a blazer, always wear makeup. You're too short. You're going to have trouble in front of a boardroom." So executive presence always had a really negative connotation; it was something that someone like me could not attain.

I really struggled with that until I came to this point of, presence is owning my power and owning how I show up. The impact I want to make. That's presence.

The more I just started owning my voice and my truth, the presence came with it.

Now that I'm an executive and I have a large leadership profile externally, I can role model what that looks like.

—Mita Mallick, bestselling author of *Reimagine Inclusion*

For mid-career professionals aiming to be seen as leaders, visibility and assertiveness are often the missing pieces. They may have the skills and experience, but they don't always clarify their strengths. I encourage my students to use labels for themselves. If you are hyper-organized, tell people. If you have a special expertise, make sure people know it. If you do not have a certain expertise, then assertively ask for help or share the task with someone who does.

—Vanessa Van Edwards, founder of ScienceofPeople.com and bestselling author

Part I: Your Career Brand

The Mindset Shift You Need to Make

It's difficult to become a leader if you don't believe that you have what it takes to be one. Imposter syndrome is just as common in the C-suite as it is for people much earlier in their careers. The key is to know the strengths you bring to the table and build your leadership style off of them.

*I think way too many leaders are trying to be everything to everyone.
Part of building your personal brand is understanding intuitively your strengths and weaknesses, which are connecting and then learning how to get relied upon for the things that you do well.*

First you have to know it about yourself, and then you can use that to build your brand with other people.

—Robert Glazer, bestselling author of *Elevate*,
Elevate Your Team, and *Friday Forward*

Reinvention can actually happen within because it's a mindset shift. Part of that can come in early as you learn and grow. For me there was this moment where I was sitting with my boss at a Mediterranean restaurant in New York. I was a new manager of ICs [individual contributors], and I never thought I would be anything beyond a line manager. He said, 'Not only do I see you getting to the next level, but I see you being an executive here,' and I was like, 'Really? Seriously?' In that moment, I saw that other people see my potential here. That's all it took, which in some ways is disheartening because why couldn't I have just seen it myself?

—Jenny Wood, author of *Wild Courage*,
former Google executive, and founder of
Google's Own Your Career program

How to Lead Authentically

As we discussed in Chapter 10, authenticity is a key expectation of today's leaders. There can be a disconnect between the traditional view of what executive presence should be and what feels authentic to you. Bridging that gap to find your authentic, sustainable leadership style will make you both more comfortable as a leader and more trustworthy to those you lead.

There are leaders who lead with authority and leaders who lead with influence. Authority can work up to a certain point, but it doesn't get you great outcomes. Leading through influence is really hard, and I think influence ultimately comes down to, do people trust you?

Are you transparent and clear in your communication? Are you clear about your motivations and why you do things and how do you build relationships?

People will respect transparency and clarity. I think that has made me come off as more authentic.

—Linda Tong, CEO of Webflow

I do think that people appreciate authenticity; they want to seek consistency. So when you say something, you say the same thing the same way across all the interactions. That's the pitfall of trying to be suddenly very corporate or very specific because you've just changed the way you're perceived.

I personally believe that consistency and how you show up is important. And executive presence, a lot of it has to do with not just how you say things, but what you say.

—Arin Bhowmick, chief design officer at SAP

How to Cultivate Trust

In Chapter 8 we showed how trust is the bedrock of your workplace relationships. The higher up the ranks you move, the more important trust becomes—without it, it becomes impossible for your team to deliver good work and align on your priorities. While earlier in your career you may have built trust naturally through your actions, as an executive it pays to become more deliberate about building trust with members of your team that you may have few one-to-one interactions with.

You have to show that whether you're a manager or an individual contributor, "Hey, I'm on your side. I want you to succeed." So giving people advice on things like how to navigate a workplace, or becoming their sponsor.

I think everyone should be a sponsor to other people to say, "Hey, I want to help you." That gives you good capital.

—Andrew Seaman, LinkedIn editor for job searches and careers

I think trust comes with building connections. So find ways to connect with people because they want to know you're human and it demonstrates vulnerability. Trust typically gets built in times where things aren't great.

There's always been books that say, "Don't mix work and your personal life." I think it's resulted in people treating colleagues as colleagues and not building friendships or not building connections.

—Linda Tong, CEO of Webflow

Why You Should Not Give Up Social Media

Some people make the mistake of thinking that sharing your work is how you move up the career ladder but then stop when they reach the higher rungs. It can also be common to think that networking only needs to happen when you need something. Social media allows others to know what you're up to, helps you stay top-of-mind, and can create extremely meaningful connections. Bonus: It's a great way to "give back" to the next generation by sharing your expertise (particularly on LinkedIn).

Our company has a really vibrant community on social media, so I'm making an effort there, despite it being really uncomfortable.

My LinkedIn presence helps people get a feel for who I am. You're doing a mix of promoting your company, recruiting, and hoping people understand who you are as a leader. The folks on there who are prospects, who either are prospective employees or are prospective customers, they use LinkedIn to better understand who is the leadership, how is this being run, what's the vision, and what exactly do you do.

—Linda Tong, CEO of Webflow

I realized that I have a lot going on with my career development and personal development and I thought, "Oh, here's a way I can maybe help more people."

—Jenny Wood, author of *Wild Courage*, former Google executive, and founder of Google's Own Your Career program

People aren't paying attention to what you're doing; you've got to get out there in public or private forums to let people know what your ideas are about your industry, about your type of work, and the projects you're focusing on. That's how they'll begin to understand where you fit and what opportunities align with your expertise and work experience.

—Brian Honigman, marketing consultant and career coach for marketers

Part II: Communication

Learn to Speak with Confidence

Part of your job as an executive is to speak on behalf of your team and the organization. As you rise in the ranks, you'll also be asked to represent the company in additional ways, like conference panels and media interviews. Continuing to invest in and improve your public speaking skills will boost the standing of everyone you represent while also increasing your credibility.

If there's one skill that, if I were to go back in time, I would put more time in, it's around communication skills—mainly around speech so that you get used to going on stage and talking.

It is important and essential to not just be successful in your career, but for you to have the presence you're talking about, to have the multiplier effect. As you go higher up, that's a gift.

In a given week, I'm having five to eight such conversations where it's not prepared remarks.

It's absolutely essential for everyone, no matter what level you are, to have some abilities to be able to speak.

—Arin Bhowmick, chief design officer at SAP

Storytelling is a critical skill because executives need to provide context. We have fireboses of data and information coming at us constantly now. Business executives need to be able to shape the data and information into stories that help people understand. AI will help us with general understanding, but it won't help with wisdom—and we gain wisdom through storytelling, which will remain a uniquely human skill.

—Brandon Carson, global development leader and author

Be Direct, Firm, and Efficient

When you become an executive, you are often communicating to many people or leading difficult, emotionally charged conversations.

Because the chances of you being misinterpreted (and the cost of being misunderstood) become higher, it's critical that you communicate as clearly—and succinctly—as possible.

As you get more senior, you're going to deal with increasingly messy problems. You have to be the one who packages it into something digestible, then show your team a path forward.

—Wes Kao, cofounder of Maven

Being able to summarize an issue succinctly and point out the key issue that you need other executives' attention or decision on—while not overwhelming them with detail—that distinguishes folks at a middle level to the more senior level.

—Christina Hall, chief people officer at Instacart

Why You Should Listen More Than Speak

Getting high-quality information is one of the hardest problems for executives, and your team plays a critical role in delivering it. Building a culture that encourages people to come forward with things they think you may not want to hear can really differentiate you as a leader. It improves the data you have to make decisions with and gives your team the psychological safety to know that they can come to you with problems without it hurting their careers. By listening without judgment you will learn more and give your team the confidence to bring you problems.

Make sure that everyone is clear that you have an open-door policy.

When people come in to speak, just listen. Don't try to respond. Don't try to think about a response because people can see it. Just kind of absorb it all.

Thank them. Maybe repeat it back to make sure you heard what you heard and then say, "Let me process this, I'll get back to you."

Now you've accomplished the first goal, which is people feel safe coming and giving you the feedback and then you can follow up afterwards.

You can decide which things you want to take or otherwise.

—Robert Glazer, bestselling author of
Elevate, Elevate Your Team, and *Friday Forward*

Watch for people who are dismissed, interrupted, talked over, or have their ideas stolen. That doesn't always happen to quiet leaders, but it can tend to happen to them. Not everyone can think quickly on their feet.

Also, follow up with people afterward: "I noticed you were quiet, but I know you have a lot of thoughts. Do you want to chat one-on-one?"

Give people an option to send thoughts and ideas in writing. That's not to say that if you are a quiet leader, you don't ever use your voice. People use their voices in different ways, and leaders need to be mindful that it can be the verbal and the nonverbal.

—Mita Mallick, business leader and *WSJ*
bestselling author of *Reimagine Inclusion*

Starting my management career, I figured out that for me to make the team better, I need to hear from people who don't want to speak up or who are afraid of being rejected or not being credible.

I noticed that some people just don't talk at all. And so then the question was, would certain one-on-ones, like social conversations, open them up? Eventually I would draw them into the conversation.

—Arin Bhowmick, chief design officer at SAP

Expert Advice on Executive Presence

Embrace Meetings

Meetings are the lifeblood of a busy executive, where you learn new information, discuss issues with your team, and make big decisions. While it's easy to have a bias against meetings (see Chapter 6), as an executive you have to commit to making them useful and productive. Making the mindset shift to ensuring you and your teams lead productive and engaging meetings is central to your (and your organization's) success.

I like to have three types of meetings.

The first are the regular cadence of leadership meetings to keep the team connected, and those are generally productive, engaging, and team building.

I also like to have meetings, sometimes every single day, on an emergency or an urgent topic. Building head count in the Middle East, how are we going to do that? We're losing business every single day. So that is a daily stand-up meeting for 30 minutes every single day until we figure it out.

And then the third type of meeting is the one where it's for a project that you need to make sure you're moving forward on a timeline. So in those I look for: What's been the progress since the last time? What are the critical issues, and where do you need my input?

—Soni Basi, global CHRO and former
global chief people officer at Edelman

Part III: Credibility

People Are Watching Your Body Language and Appearance

Becoming an executive means that the spotlight on you shines a little brighter than before. This means more than your words will be scrutinized; people will pick up signals from your body language and clothing, so you need to make sure you're sending out the signals you want. The brighter the spotlight, the more every detail is revealed and put under the microscope, so you'll want to sweat the details to communicate the right message.

Body language is my favorite tool for conveying confidence and leadership. Whether in person or on a virtual call, maintaining an open posture, making appropriate eye contact, and using deliberate gestures can signal you are confident and in control. I also love a lower lid flex, which shows contemplation. A great way to dial up competence is to speak with a downward inflection and use precise numbers when explaining points or ideas.

Charismatic leaders often excel in clear and concise communication. They use hyper-specific hand gestures, they make more eye contact, and they use the lowest end of their natural voice tone.

—Vanessa Van Edwards, founder of
ScienceofPeople.com and bestselling author

I focus on actively trying to understand how people are feeling or how they're reacting to things and then adjusting accordingly.

Body language or reading facial expressions comes into play through a lot of things I do. I don't look at presentations when we're in meetings and people are presenting slides, I listen and I look at other people's reactions.

—Linda Tong, CEO of Webflow

Why Leaders Have to Understand Bias

It's important to recognize that bias always exists, usually unconsciously. Without acknowledging and working to understand your own biases—and those of the people you work with—it becomes impossible to make high-quality decisions that are fair and equitable. Listening to the voices of those who may be the victims of bias is one of the best ways to understand what you aren't seeing and how to begin to level the playing field. This is especially true for the "only" person in the room—whether it's being the only woman, the only person of color, or the only introvert, the feeling can be isolating and overwhelming.

Our parents and our grandparents grew up in extremely turbulent times, so they naturally value security and stability.

When you are taught to overvalue stability and security, it often leads to deprioritizing certain types of ambition, because ambition equals risk and risk is the opposite of stability.

After my Korean grandparents were born in Japanese occupation and had to fight for their own independence and my parents made the decision to come to start a new life in a foreign country, it's hard for me to accept that I am to stay silent, whether at school, work, or in the community.

That doesn't compute. I'm not honoring them, and centuries of their risk-taking and resilience, if I let myself be taken advantage of, ignored, and be overlooked for promotion. It's in my DNA to stand up for myself and others.

It's my responsibility to now build upon the contributions of my ancestors and to redefine what I am capable of achieving, making good on their sacrifices.

—Jerry Won, founder of World Class Speakers

I find it less helpful to think about diversity as this 30,000-foot topic. I think it can be much more clarifying to focus on real brass tacks issues of, "I'm in a room with someone; how do I make that person feel comfortable?"

—Dorie Clark, *WSJ* bestselling author of *The Long Game*

Unforgettable Presence

Why You Can't Stop Managing Up

People have the misconception that you need to focus on your manager less as you move up the ranks. Even in the C-suite, the priorities of the person you report to (whether that be the CEO or the board of directors) have an outsized influence on your own success. You'll need to become adept at not only understanding your boss' priorities but showing how you and your team's work contributes to the bigger picture.

A common myth is once you hit a certain level in your career, you don't have to manage up anymore. But senior people are actually the best at managing up. This is part of the reason they got to where they are in the first place. The more senior you are, the more you need to make assertions about what to do and get what you need from others to make it happen—without your manager explicitly telling you what to do each step of the way.

—Wes Kao, cofounder of Maven

Managing up comes down to relationships. In my particular role, while I may not work directly with executives who are above my leader specifically, I am working directly with the teams that support them.

This is my sandbox now, these folks who support these leaders. That's a less intimidating way to get closer to an executive or a leader who you want to get to know better.

Having a good reputation and working with those folks who have the influence and have the ear of the leader is definitely my approach in terms of how you manage up.

—Carlo Dela Fuente,
chief of staff, director of Business Operations for
Webex Product Management and Artificial Intelligence at Cisco

Expert Advice on Executive Presence

Strategy and Decision-Making

As an executive, your responsibilities become more about setting strategy than executing on it. Learning how to make and explain decisions confidently will shape many people's impression of your performance.

There is a phenomenon in the psychological literature called Solomon's Paradox, where we tend to be very good at making decisions, but not so good at making decisions about our own self.

So there's some self-distancing techniques that you can use to be bolder. For instance, suppose you're contemplating speaking up in a meeting, and you're not sure what to do.

One thing you can do is ask yourself, "If my best friend came to me right now with this question of what to do, what would I tell her to do?"

You can also imagine having a conversation with yourself 10 years from now. What is one year or five years from now like?

What would the person from one year or five years from now want you to do? What do you want to tell the one-year or five-years-from-now person?

You want to tell the person a year or five years from now that you stood up and tried something.

—Daniel Pink, author of five *NYT* bestsellers
including *Drive* and *The Power of Regret*

Relationship building will always be needed to build someone's confidence to move from mid-manager to senior leadership: understanding the differences between critical thinking and strategic thinking; being able to understand profit-and-loss statements and budgeting; the ability to manage individuals and have them manage you; the ability to have a strong voice and a futurist voice about where the business is going; the ability to see multiple pathways to achieve the same result.

—H Walker, vice president and human-centered strategies officer, Boys & Girls Clubs of America

With innovation and strategy, it's really sitting down, stepping back and understanding what are the problems facing our customers in the world.

After framing what we are trying to solve, it's then going, "Why is that the case?" and then going, "Let's be completely out there, remove all the rules, all the constraints, let's be, some might say crazy, in thinking about this space.

Then play it out, and don't just play it out to the one round, play it out a few rounds.

—Brendan Ittelson, chief ecosystem officer at Zoom

Expert Advice on Executive Presence

Conclusion

An Unforgettable Future

You've put in the work. Your LinkedIn presence sparkles, you're a meeting master, and you've deepened your relationships up and down the org chart. What does the future hold for you?

The exciting part about developing your presence is that you can't predict where it will take you—although I'm confident it will be somewhere exciting! When I began—a shy yet ambitious professional who thrived doing heads-down work—I never would have imagined that I'd end up as a keynote speaker and entrepreneur. Most people are not going to go this route—that's okay, you have your own dream that you're trying to achieve. Perhaps it's to become part of the C-suite. Maybe you want to lead a team (I had the same dream and it was so fulfilling!). What's important to remember is that whatever path you choose, your professional presence will be critical to helping you reach those goals.

This transformation can feel abstract and far away when you're just starting out, so let me share some concrete examples:

- *Example 1*

  By developing a strong virtual presence, and honing her virtual presentation skills, Ivana (in Chapter 2) won the pitch competition and became a Stanford Fellow.

- *Example 2*

  *For my client, Mandy, who was recently promoted to sales man-
  ager, she was asked by her manager to practice her "executive
  presence." She eliminated uptalk in her communication and
  created a thoughtful, well-rehearsed, visually engaging
  presentation—making her feel more confident and appear
  more credible to senior stakeholders.*

- *Example 3*

  *For Jean Kang, she found her voice and grew her confidence
  through taking on the challenge of posting regularly on LinkedIn.*

- *Example 4*

  *By understanding how to take ownership of my career and be
  more intentional with my professional presence, I got promoted
  quickly and eventually created a new career path for myself.*

I want you to come away from reading this book feeling inspired
and ready to show the world what you can do. High achievers (like
you!) are often very motivated to keep learning new things and
pushing yourself to get to the next level. Communications expert
Vinh Giang has seen this with his students. They're very motivated,
but they can also fall into the trap of focusing on learning more than
applying what they've learned.

"Some have an addiction to knowledge acquisition. They can't
get enough of learning more tips, more tricks, more podcasts, but
they don't apply any of it. I'm trying to get them to be more addicted
to knowledge application," says Vinh. "The students that start applying what they've learned, they start to get addicted to that because
that's where the results live."

Picking one thing per day to work on is a great way to move toward knowledge application. But I'd be lying if I said there won't be other obstacles along the way. The hardest ones to overcome are the obstacles inside you. Fear and doubt are partners on this journey, but the goal of this book is to give you the tools, frameworks, and expert advice to overcome them. Focusing on the concrete, actionable steps I've shared in this book will help you quiet the negative voices in your head in almost any situation—or at least make you realize that you don't need to listen to them.

Still, challenges will sometimes come up that slow your progress. This could be many things, but I want to talk about two common ones.

The first is when you lose your job unexpectedly. Unfortunately, this will happen to most people at some point in their careers. It hurts! It feels unfair and it can undermine your confidence. I know because it happened to me.

It's hard to want to grow your presence in these moments, but it's exactly what you need to do to move on to the next fantastic opportunity. While it can feel like you're alone, your network will often guide you to your next job. Remember that your LinkedIn presence gives you the ability to reach out and get that informational interview that will open doors or help you learn about a new industry. When you do land an interview for your dream role, you'll be equipped to show up professionally on camera, and your career brand will give you a great story to tell and the confidence to speak powerfully about your abilities and accomplishments.

"A personal brand is the only thing that's going to be bulletproof through layoffs and it's going to get you the visibility and the connections you need to go forward," says Jess Ramos, a senior data analyst in tech and the founder of Big Data Energy Analytics. "Your brand literally lasts forever. It's the one part of your career you can always take with you."

When I was laid off from Prezi, I didn't know what would come next. It was late 2022 and part of me was tempted to take the first job

I could find so that I could feel secure and validated as a professional. But it was my network—mentors, past colleagues, and friends—who gave me the confidence to leap into the unknown and start my own business. It was the presence I had built and continued to expand. The years I'd spent becoming the CEO of my career helped me believe that I could be the CEO of my company.

The other worry that many knowledge workers have is the shadow of AI. For some people, they're nervous that something is coming that will eventually replace them.

Fortunately for us, presence is the one thing that an AI can't have. AI does not have a story that allows it to connect with others, it doesn't know how to influence stakeholders, and it can't deliver an inspiring talk. Leaning into the things that strengthen your presence are exactly the skills you need to stand out in a sea of algorithmically generated information.

Working with AI is also a skill you can develop like any other. It can be a useful research assistant for your next presentation. It can help you come up with ideas for LinkedIn posts. Used correctly, it can actually be a tool that helps you amplify your presence.

"The real opportunity I see is having humans and their algorithmic counterparts making joint decisions and dividing up tasks based on, 'Where is a piece of AI more effective and where is a person more effective?'" says Alexandra Levit, global workplace futurist and author of *Deep Talent*. "Every job is being redesigned, or should be being redesigned, with that in mind."

I hope that one of your takeaways from this book is that you have to constantly be evolving and upgrading your skills. There really is no finish line when it comes to growth. Continue to be intentional about learning new things and applying those learnings.

"I think a lot of professionals are still very married to the old idea of a career trajectory. People either think they graduated college with everything they're going to ever need to know, or that they've been working for so long that they couldn't possibly know anything else," says Andrew Seaman, LinkedIn editor for job searches and careers. "But the truth is, you have to be willing to say, 'I don't know what the future is going to hold and I have to be nimble and open to learning.' As long as you're malleable and open to education and changes, I think you'll have a much longer and fulfilling career."

While it may feel overwhelming, think of it this way: Every small step you take is helping you build confidence. It's helping you create that unforgettable presence. And it's setting you up for success no matter what you choose to do.

If you're a manager or executive, this is why you have to be constantly investing in training and educational opportunities for your team. According to a Gallup poll, 87% of millennials say that professional development or career growth opportunities are important to them.[1] It will not only keep your team current with the skills they need to succeed, but it will help them feel more confident about facing the future as your organization adapts.

"The thing with the future is that nothing's off the table because crazy things happen all the time. Employees are concerned about career durability, which means the ability to remain gainfully employed over a continuous period of time, despite automation or something that's rendering a part of their job obsolete," says Levit. "They're nervous about whether they'll be able to upskill."

As someone reading this book, you've already taken steps to take control of your future. As a leader, it's your responsibility to make sure those opportunities are available to everyone on your team and that you provide them with the resources necessary to embrace a learning mindset.

■　■　■

It's no coincidence that I named my company RISE Learning Solutions. I believe that investing in continuous learning is the shortest path to giving anyone the ability to "rise." For me, RISE has a very specific meaning—to help others be more recognized, influential, successful, and empowered, no matter what you are trying to achieve.

In writing this book, I hope I've helped you on your own learning journey. By embracing the tips and skills shared by me and the many experts I've spoken with, I want you to feel like you can take on any challenge. Developing your presence is ultimately a tool to help you build the career and future that you want—or maybe even catapult you farther than you even thought possible.

Whatever your path is, I want you to feel like you're in charge of it. Building your professional presence will not only make you unforgettable to others but, by becoming the CEO of your career, empower you to create a future that will be unforgettable for you as well.

Please send me updates on your journey, I would really love to hear from you. Send me a connection request on LinkedIn (with a note!), I'd be thrilled to accept it. I'd also love to speak, teach, or coach people at your organization, so drop me a note at contact@ lorraineklee.com if you'd like to work together and dive deeper into the ideas from this book.

Whatever you decide to do, I look forward to seeing you, wherever you decide to make your presence felt.

Contact Me

Your success story could inspire others! Have you created an unforgettable presence using insights from this book? I'd love to celebrate your journey and share it with others.

Drop me a note at book@lorraineklee.com. *Your experience could be featured in my newsletter or social media, helping others see what's possible.*

I look forward to hearing from you!

Let's collaborate!

I hope this book has served as a helpful and energizing guide to support you and your teams in building your unforgettable presence! If you'd like to dive deeper with me to expand on the topics in this book, I work with Fortune 500 companies, universities, and more through memorable keynotes and hands-on training programs that drive lasting results.

Signature offerings:

- High-impact keynotes that inspire immediate action
- Comprehensive training programs with practical, hands-on learning
- Interactive trainings for distributed teams
- Executive coaching for high-stakes presentations
- Consulting for impactful LinkedIn strategies
- Strategic communication advisory services
- Customized on-demand courses

I also offer virtual and in-person collaborations for:

- VIP events
- Sales trainings
- Annual meetings
- Manager programs
- New-hire orientations
- Employee resource group sessions

My approach focuses on practical, actionable strategies that participants can implement immediately (and oftentimes during the session itself!). Event organizers, audience members, and executive clients consistently highlight how my sessions bring a combination of tactical content and an engaging delivery. In post-event surveys across hundreds of sessions—from hourlong keynotes to multiweek programs—participants consistently report gaining valuable new tools, frameworks, and strategies that they apply right away.

Many organizations start with an energizing keynote to build momentum, followed by an in-depth training program to further cement those skills and receive more personalized feedback from me.

Let's discuss how we can best partner to support your organization's specific goals and culture.

Ready to elevate your team's presence and impact? **Contact me at contact@lorraineklee.com to chat!**

Acronyms and Frameworks

Chapter 1

- EPIC career brand: Experiences, Personality, Identity, Community
- UPI: Unique and Powerful Introduction

Chapter 2

- TEA Method: Tech, Energy, Aesthetics

Chapter 3

- Stage 1: Explore
- Stage 2: Establish
- Stage 3: Envision
- Stage 4: Excel

Chapter 5

- The Presentation Attention Toolbox
  - Hook people's attention right away
  - Understand your audience
  - Add rapid movement

- Use arresting visuals
- Vary your voice
- Communicate with your body
- Finish with a strong conclusion

Chapter 6

- The Passive to Active Meeting Framework
  - Warm up
  - Invite participation
  - Pause
  - Listen and observe
  - Move the conversation forward

Chapter 8

- RAVE Model: Relationships, Appearances, Visibility, Expertise

Chapter 9

- The Three Rs of receiving feedback: Request, Reflect, Respond

Chapter 11

- FOCUS Framework
  - Frame it
  - Observe it
  - Consequences
  - Understand it
  - Steps to take

Acronyms and Frameworks

Notes

Introduction: What Does It Mean to Be Unforgettable?

1. "Benefits of online employee training." LinkedIn Learning. https://learning.linkedin.com/resources/career-development/online-employee-training-benefits#:~:text=The%20number%20one%20reason%20employees,in%20their%20learning%20and%20development.

Chapter 1 Crafting Your Career Brand

1. Burkus, David. "If You Want to Be the Boss, Say 'We' Not 'I.'" *Harvard Business Review*, March 6, 2015. https://hbr.org/2015/03/if-you-want-to-be-the-boss-say-we-not-i

2. Hewlett, Sylvia Ann. "The new rules of executive presence." *Harvard Business Review*, January/February 2024. https://hbr.org/2024/01/the-new-rules-of-executive-presence

3. Wood, Jenny. *Wild Courage: Go after what you want and get it*. Penguin Random House. March 25, 2025.

Chapter 2 Turning Video Into Your Superpower

1. Cook, Abi, Meg Thompson, Paddy Ross, Pat Barclay. "Virtual First Impressions: Zoom Backgrounds Affect Judgements of Trust and Competence." *PLoS One*, September 27, 2023. https://www.ncbi.nlm.nih.gov/pmc/articles/PMC10529556/.

2. Wargo, Eric. "How many seconds to a first impression?" *Association for Psychological Science*, July 1, 2006. https://www.psychologicalscience.org/observer/how-many-seconds-to-a-first-impression

3. Gregoire, Carolyn. "The fascinating science behind 'talking' with your hands." *Huffington Post*, February 4, 2016. https://www.huffpost.com/entry/talking-with-hands-gestures_n_56afcfaae4b0b8d7c230414e

4. Burkus, David. "If You Want to Be the Boss, Say 'We' Not 'I.'" *Harvard Business Review*, March 06, 2015. https://hbr.org/2015/03/if-you-want-to-be-the-boss-say-we-not-i.

5. Lynch, Hallie, Noah Zandan. "Dress for the (Remote) Job You Want." *Harvard Business Review,* June 18, 2020. https://hbr.org/2020/06/dress-for-the-remote-job-you-want.

6. Cook, Abi, Meg Thompson, Paddy Ross, Pat Barclay. "Virtual First Impressions: Zoom Backgrounds Affect Judgements of Trust and Competence." *PLoS One*, September 27, 2023. https://www.ncbi.nlm.nih.gov/pmc/articles/PMC10529556/.

7. Bailenson, Jeremy. "Nonverbal overload: A theoretical argument for the causes of Zoom fatigue." *Technology, Mind and Behavior,* Vol 2, Issue 1. https://tmb.apaopen.org/pub/nonverbal-overload/release/2

8. Grassini, Simone. "A systematic review and meta-analysis of nature walk as an intervention for anxiety and depression." *Journal of Clinical Medicine*, March 21, 2022. https://www.ncbi.nlm.nih.gov/pmc/articles/PMC8953618/

Chapter 3 Using LinkedIn the Right Way

1. Shepherd, Jack. "41 Essential LinkedIn Statistics You Need to Know in 2024." *The Social Shepherd*, April 23, 2024. https://thesocialshepherd.com/blog/linkedin-statistics

2. LinkedIn. "Powerful Recruiting Tools." Accessed August 06, 2024. https://business.linkedin.com/talent-solutions.

3. Schultz, Mike. "6 common LinkedIn selling mistakes and how to avoid them." rainsalestraining.com https://www.rainsalestraining.com/blog/6-common-linkedin-selling-mistakes-and-how-to-avoid-them

4. Burt, Tequia. "13 Ways to Boost the Impact of Your LinkedIn Page the Rest of 2024." *LinkedIn*, August 9, 2024. https://www.linkedin.com/business/marketing/blog/linkedin-pages/5-non-obvious-ways-to-improve-your-linkedin-company-page

Chapter 4 Becoming a Confident Communicator

1. Langer, Ellen, Arthur Blank, and Benzion Chanowitz. "The Mindlessness of Ostensibly Thoughtful Action: The Role of 'Placebic' Information in Interpersonal Interaction." *Journal of Personality and Social Psychology*, 1978, 6th ed., 36:635–42.
2. Fiske, Susan T., Amy J.C. Cuddy, and Peter Glick. "Universal Dimensions of Social Cognition: Warmth and Competence." *Trends in Cognitive Sciences* 11, no. 2 (February 2007): 77–83. https://doi.org/10.1016/j.tics.2006.11.005.
3. Spicer, Andre. "How many work emails is too many?" *The Guardian*, April 8, 2019. https://www.theguardian.com/technology/shortcuts/2019/apr/08/how-many-work-emails-is-too-many
4. Cleveland Clinic. "What Is the Fight, Flight, Freeze or Fawn Response?" Last modified July 22, 2024. https://health.clevelandclinic.org/what-happens-to-your-body-during-the-fight-or-flight-response.

Chapter 5 Supercharging Your Virtual Presentations

1. LaMotte, Sandy. "If you think you can't focus for long, you're right." *CNN*, May 15, 2024. https://www.cnn.com/2023/01/11/health/short-attention-span-wellness/index.html
2. Jawed, Soyiba, Hafeez Ullah Amin, Aamir Saeed Malik, and Ibrahima Faye. "Classification of Visual and Non-Visual Learners Using Electroencephalographic Alpha and Gamma Activities." *Frontiers in Behavioral Neuroscience* 13 (May 7, 2019). https://doi.org/10.3389/fnbeh.2019.00086

3. Van Edwards, Vanessa. "The science of eating." *Huffington Post,* June 16, 2015. https://www.huffpost.com/entry/science-of-eating_b_7497592

4. Harvard Medical School. "Learning Diaphragmatic Breathing." *Harvard Health Publishing*, March 10, 2016. https://www.health.harvard.edu/healthbeat/learning-diaphragmatic-breathing

5. D. Edwards, Vanessa Van, and Brandon Vaughn. "5 Secrets of a Successful TED Talk." *Science of People*, July 1, 2024. https://www.scienceofpeople.com/secrets-of-a-successful-ted-talk/#:~:text=Our%20hands%20are%20a%20nonverbal,an%20easier%20time%20understanding%20them

Chapter 6 Leading Meetings That Are Actually Good

1. Rogelberg, Steven. "The cost of unnecessary meeting attendance." Published by Otter.ai, September 26, 2022. https://www.businesswire.com/news/home/20220926005145/en/One-third-of-Meetings-Are-Unnecessary-Costing-Companies-Millions-and-No-One-Is-Happy-About-It

2. Future Forum. "Inflexible Return-to-Office Policies Are Hammering Employee Experience Scores." Last modified April 19, 2022. https://futureforum.com/wp-content/uploads/2022/04/Future-Forum-Pulse-Report-April-2022.pdf

3. Dahl, Melissa. "Four seconds is all it takes for silence to get awkward." *NBC News,* January 27, 2011. https://www.nbcnews.com/health/body-odd/four-seconds-all-it-takes-silence-get-awkward-flna1c6437340

Chapter 7 Making Yourself Unforgettable to Executives

1. Wargo, Eric. "How many seconds to a first impression?" *Association for Psychological Science*, July 1, 2006. https://www.psychologicalscience.org/observer/how-many-seconds-to-a-first-impression

2. Grant, Adam. "How to trust people you don't like." LinkedIn, May 7, 2018. https://www.linkedin.com/pulse/how-trust-people-you-dont-like-adam-grant/

Chapter 8 Building Influence at Any Level

1. Patel, Alok, Stephanie Plowman. "The increasing importance of a best friend at work." Gallup.com, August 17, 2022. https://www.gallup.com/workplace/397058/increasing-importance-best-friend-work.aspx
2. "Bucking the trend: Asian employees job satisfaction in the U.S. workplace." Asia Society 2019 Asian Corporate Survey. https://asiasociety.org/sites/default/files/2019-05/2019%20Asian%20Corporate%20Survey%20Executive%20Summary.pdf

Chapter 9 Managing Your Manager

1. "LinkedIn Talent Solutions." March 5, 2019. https://business.linkedin.com/content/dam/me/business/en-us/talent-solutions-lodestone/body/pdf/Gender-Insights-Report.pdf
2. Li, Danielle, Alan Benson, Kelly Shue. "Potential and the gender promotion gap." June 22, 2022. https://danielle-li.github.io/assets/docs/PotentialAndTheGenderPromotionGap.pdf

Chapter 10 Thinking Like a Manager

1. "Executives feel the strain of leading in the 'new normal'." Future Forum Pulse Survey, October 2022. https://futureforum.com/wp-content/uploads/2022/10/Future-Forum-Pulse-Report-Fall-2022.pdf
2. Ryback, Ralph. "The science of accomplishing your goals." *Psychology Today*, October 3, 2016. https://www.psychologytoday.com/ca/blog/the-truisms-wellness/201610/the-science-accomplishing-your-goals

Chapter 11 Increasing Your Team's Presence

1. Solomon, Lou. "Two-thirds of managers are uncomfortable communicating with employees." *Harvard Business Review*, March 9, 2016. https://hbr.org/2016/03/two-thirds-of-managers-are-uncomfortable-communicating-with-employees

2. Yildirim, Ece. "Get rid of the feedback sandwich—use this 1 sentence instead." CNBC.com, December 13, 2023. https://www.cnbc.com/2023/12/13/adam-grant-feedback-sandwiches-dont-work-use-this-sentence-instead.html

Chapter 12 Expert Advice on Executive Presence

1. Hewlett, Sylvia Ann. "The new rules of executive presence." *Harvard Business Review*, January/February 2024. https://hbr.org/2024/01/the-new-rules-of-executive-presence

Conclusion: An Unforgettable Future

1. Hickman, Adam. "What 'meaningful feedback' means to millennials." Gallup Workplace, January 29, 2020. https://www.gallup.com/workplace/284081/meaningful-feedback-means-millennials.aspx#:~:text=Gallup%20research%20shows%20that%2087,up%20and%20ask%20for%20feedback.

Acknowledgments

When it became official that I was writing this book, one of the things I was most excited to do was write this acknowledgments section. All the stories and advice in this book are a culmination of so many experiences and relationships built over my decades-plus career that have made this possible.

First and foremost, I need to thank the person who gave me the idea to write a book in the first place, Arun J! Like we saw in some of the stories shared, having a manager, friend, or mentor who sees the potential in you even before you see it in yourself can be life-changing. I'm so appreciative that Arun planted this idea in my head. Publishing this book has been a career highlight.

I'd also like to thank my editor, Neill Brian, whose initial LinkedIn message asking if I had ever thought about writing a book had me jumping out of my chair in excitement (This is just one example of the opportunities that can come your way when you have a strong LinkedIn presence!). I'd also like to thank the rest of the team at Wiley, including editorial assistant Gabriela Mancuso, who was always so responsive and quick to answer my (many) questions.

Writing a book takes a team, and I had the best one! Thank you to Gene Shannon, my book coach, for being an important sounding board and for helping me make sense of my many ideas. My beta readers (Amara Hoshijo, Casey Zanowicz, Gloria Zhu, Lindsay Traiman, and Min Fang) also provided invaluable feedback; I know how smart you all are, and it was inspiring and energizing to see you in action. I'd also like to thank my former colleague Michael Lee, who was the person I trusted most to copyedit my work when we were coworkers and continues to be that person today. I am also so appreciative of my coaching clients, students, and the organizations that have brought me in to speak and work with their teams. I've learned so much from you, and you make me better at what I do!

One of the best parts of this job is how many interesting and accomplished people I get to meet, including many other keynote speakers and authors. I appreciate all of you for sharing your candid advice with me about different aspects of the book process and for introductions that you made. One of those people was fellow author Martin Gonzalez, whom I met after he sent me a LinkedIn message to introduce himself. After meeting virtually only once, Martin offered to lead a one-hour group "book title brainstorming session." I don't think he anticipated the number of WhatsApp messages that would get sent to him as we all continued brainstorming, but I'm eternally grateful he was so patient and generous with his time to a complete stranger (I'm lucky to now call him a friend!). His input was invaluable in coming up with the title of this book.

I interviewed nearly three dozen business leaders and professionals at the top of their fields, and I'm beyond appreciative of all of them for being so willing to share their stories, insights, and time with me. I learned something new from each of you and thoroughly enjoyed every call.

A few of those individuals are those who have been so generous with their knowledge and experience over the past few years. My former colleague Spencer Waldron, whose superb public speaking skills inspired me to get more comfortable with my own, agreed to coach me—something outside of his job description. It was his encouragement and feedback that ultimately started me on the journey I'm on now. Another is Matt Abrahams, who was the speaker coach at a conference I spoke at. Matt offered to stay in touch after that initial meeting and has been someone who continues to uplift voices and faces that haven't historically been invited to speak on stages—the world needs more advocates like him. Rich Mulholland is another mentor who has given me feedback on my speaking, unprompted, out of the goodness of his heart to help me improve and has continued to be very candid with me whenever I have questions about the business side of speaking.

To my husband (and volunteer CFO), Min, thank you so much for your continued love, support, and encouragement, and for being my most trusted business advisor. Your belief in me has allowed me to build a career and business shaped around the life we want to lead.

I have so much deep gratitude for my parents and my sister, Justine, who have always been a supportive, loving, and grounding force in my life, no matter the path I chose to take—from studying journalism to jumping into tech to now building my own company. Justine in particular has done so much for my business (and the book!), especially when I first started off—she created logos and designs, reviewed my LinkedIn content when I was nervous to hit "post," sent countless content ideas, and so much more, all while juggling her full-time job. I'm so lucky to have you all in my corner!

Last but certainly not least, thank you to you, the reader, for picking up this book and for putting your trust in me to help you along this journey of building your unforgettable presence. I'm so thankful for your support, and I can't wait to see what you do next!

About the Author

Lorraine K. Lee is a highly sought-after keynote speaker and the founder of RISE Learning Solutions.

A former founding editor at companies such as LinkedIn and Prezi, Lorraine brings unique expertise in empowering both high-potential and established leaders to supercharge their presence, influence, and impact. She is passionate about helping ambitious professionals go from invisible to unforgettable in the modern workplace.

Her frameworks, like the TEA Method and RAVE Model, have been adopted by Fortune 500 companies and other globally recognized organizations including Zoom, Amazon, Cisco, and McKinsey & Company.

With hundreds of thousands of LinkedIn followers, she is recognized as a LinkedIn Top Voice in workplace communication and presence. When Lorraine isn't speaking, she teaches popular courses at Stanford Continuing Studies and LinkedIn Learning that reach a large global audience.

Lorraine's insights have been featured in media outlets including *CNBC, Forbes, Inc., Bloomberg, Fast Company,* and *Entrepreneur.* She lives in San Francisco with her husband.

Connect with Lorraine: www.lorraineklee.com

LinkedIn: linkedin.com/in/lorraineklee

Instagram/Threads: @lorraineklee

Index

249

Index

254

Index